THE PRYMER

THE PRYMER

THE PRAYER BOOK OF THE MEDIAEVAL ERA
ADAPTED FOR CONTEMPORARY USE

Translated and Adapted by
Robert Webber

SPCK

Published in Great Britain in 2000 by
Society for Promoting Christian Knowledge
Holy Trinity Church
Marylebone Road
London NW1 4DU

First published in the USA in 2000 by
Paraclete Press, Brewster, Massachusetts, USA.
www.paracletepress.com

British Library Cataloguing-in-Publication Data

A catalogue record for this book is available from the British Library

ISBN 0-281-05407-X

Contents

II. PRAYERS AND READINGS FOR A TIME OF GRIEF

Acknowledgments

A book cannot be prepared without dependence on a host of people who contribute to the primary author or editor. I am keenly aware of that reality and want to acknowledge those who have participated in this project.

Thanks belongs to Wheaton College where I was teaching at the time. Recognizing the value of this project, the administration gave me a sabbatical from my teaching to concentrate on research in the fifteenth century and in the translation of *The Prymer*. The school also provided additional monies from the G.W. Aldeen Memorial Fund to help with the work of translation. I especially want to thank my colleague Dr. Arthur Rupprecht from the Foreign Language department for his expertise in the translation of Latin phrases and texts. I want to acknowledge the special work of my assistant, Sydney Rhind-Westrate, with the Chaucerian English and adaptation to contemporary language. Thanks, too, to Carmen Martinez, my assistant at the Institute for Worship Studies, for her work at the computer. Finally, I want to thank my editor at Paraclete Press, Robert Edmonson, whose expertise in Latin as well as his sense of translation has made the text much more consistent and readable. All these people have made my workload lighter and contributed significantly to this publication!

The unique little book that you hold in your hands, the *Prymer*, is a product of the medieval era. For thousands of deeply devout Christians in the fifteenth century, it was the primary source of spirituality and prayer.

BACKGROUND

The origin of the *Prymer* lies in the monasteries of the ninth and tenth centuries. Here various parts of the *Prymer* originated as additional prayers to the daily prescribed prayer. After several hundred years of evolution these prayers were adopted by the clergy of the churches and used as a spiritual guide within the church for the clerical staff. Eventually lay folk began to use these prayers for private devotions and for teaching the young how to read. By the fifteenth century thousands of carefully hand-copied manuscripts of these prayers, known as the *Prymer* (first prayers), were used daily by those who could read. After the emergence of the Gutenberg Press and then the Renaissance and the Reformation of the sixteenth century, the *Prymer* was replaced in England by the *Book of Common Prayer* and by the rise of the *Catechism* movement in both Catholic and Protestant churches.

While various arrangements of the *Prymers* existed, it is commonly recognized that these *Prymers* were characterized by a strong similarity of content. For this reason we are justified in saying that there is only one *Prymer* common to the Middle Ages. When we pray this *Prymer* we are joining with thousands of fifteenth-century committed Christians who prayed these prayers daily or in the cycle of the Christian year, particularly Advent and Lent.

The first part of the *Prymer*, which I have called "Prayers and Readings for Daily Devotion," was originally called the "Hours of the Blessed Virgin." They are really the hours of the last day of Jesus. While Marian theology was quite prominent in the fifteenth century (as reflected in the title of the Hours), the Hours are focused on Jesus from the perspective of his mother. These prayers constitute the daily prayers of medieval spirituality.

In addition to the daily hours of prayer, a second section of all *Prymers* is the Office of the Dead. I have called these "Prayers and Readings for a Time of Grief." These prayers were said at a death, at a funeral, and in private. During the medieval era the black plague took thousands of lives. Premature death was a common occurrence in every city, village, and hamlet. These prayers of death gave the people a Christian way to think about death, to mourn the passing of their loved ones, and to prepare for their own death.

The *Prymer* prayers are by no means detached and uninvolved rituals. They burn with the passion characteristic of the fifteenth-century church in England. Sixty-three psalms are common to all the *Prymers* in various countries and are regarded as the most popular psalms of the medieval period. Numerous people, especially those who could not read, memorized these psalms.

Ruminato

The most widely used method of prayer in fifteenth-century England was known as *ruminato*. The meaning of the word is "to consider, to meditate upon, to ingest and to chew upon."

Ruminato was a new form of prayer destined to flourish in the fifteenth century. Daily prayers were said in common in the church. But the burst of lay spirituality in the fifteenth century took the Daily Prayer of the communal setting and privatized it for personal lay spirituality. Spirituality became a highly personalized, interior, and spontaneous devotion.

The *ruminato* way of praying replaced the *Lectio Divina* of monastic spirituality with its emphasis on reason and external understanding of the text. It moved spiritual reflection from an objective reflection on the text to a concern for how the text formed the person.

This new concern for personal spirituality is evident in the *Prymer* fragments that remain from the fifteenth century. Many of these fragments contain personal spiritual comments and prayers written in the margins of the manuscript by lay people as they prayed and ruminated on the text.

The *Prymer* is particularly useful for the twenty-first century because we are undergoing a similar shift from the emphasis on objective truth to a desire for a more subjective experience of truth. Reason, external rituals and standards characterized modernity (1750–1990). Postmodernity (1990–present) is characterized by the inner disciplines. People want to own the truth and have their personal subjective experience of truth.

This trend can be seen, for example, in the current interpretation of literature known as the "Reader-response Theory." The objective nature of the literary piece is subsumed to the personal subjective experience of the reader. What the reader takes away from the encounter with the literary piece is most important.

Ruminato is like the reader-response theory in that it emphasizes the personal inner response, the desire to claim the Scripture for oneself and to embrace its teaching in such a way that it speaks to the moment at hand. Of course, in the Christian tradition we have a communal authority in the teachings of the church. This authority does not need to be denied. It keeps our personal response in check so that we do not fall into wrong teachings because of our desire to have a personal experience.

For example, one of my classes was discussing the matter of *ruminato*. A student gave the following example: "My young adults," he said, "were discussing a psalm. I asked them to respond to the question, 'What is God saying to you in this passage?' One student said, 'I'm particularly struck by the phrase, "and David sat down." I hear God saying to me, "Jane, you are too busy, you need to slow down, take some time away from your busy life to meditate, pray and reflect."' My student asked, 'How do you respond to this statement? This certainly wasn't what David had in mind, was it?' My answer was this: 'There is nothing in this interpretation that contradicts either the universally held doctrine of the church or the morality of Christian ethics. If you don't allow a person to hear God in Scripture in a way that doesn't contradict the church's teaching, then you have taken the Scripture away from the people and put it all into the hands of the scholars and the communal consensus of the Church. Encourage your people to know the teaching of the church and yet, at the same time, to be open to the personal voice of God in Scripture as God illumines words of direction and comforts the reader in his or her own specific life situation. This is *ruminato*.'"

In keeping with the *ruminato* of the fifteenth century, I have designed a space on the right side of each page, where, like the devout of the fifteenth century, you may record your own spiritual experience with the text. I have also made brief comments that will guide your reflection on the text.

This *Prymer*, the most widely used form of spirituality in the fifteenth century, could become a standard for the inner spiritual life of the lay folk of the twenty-first century as well. So commit yourself to the daily prayers and ruminate in Scripture and prayer to the health of your inner person.

PRAYERS AND READINGS FOR
Daily Devotion

What I have called the *Prayers and Readings for Daily Devotion* were called *The Hours of the Blessed Virgin Mary* or often just the *Book of Hours* in the *Prymers* of the fifteenth century.

Essentially, the *Book of Hours* was a series of short services to be said at various hours throughout the day. These services were modeled on the hours of prayer in monasteries and adapted for use by lay people. This lay people's prayer book follows the same daily pattern of prayer used in the monastery—Matins, Lauds, Prime, Terce, Sext, None, Vespers, and Compline—but is considerably shorter and simpler, and contains fewer variable readings and prayers.

One can see immediately that the genius of the *Book of Hours* is that it integrated the prayer life of the clergy and the lay people. All God's people were united in doing similar prayers at the same time throughout the day. These prayers were not done by only a few people here and there but by a vast multitude. Copies of the *Prymer* were made available in the thousands. Some were beautifully illuminated manuscripts, while others were small volumes with little or no decoration at all.

The *Book of Hours* is essentially organized around the theology of creation, incarnation, death, and resurrection. The praise of God for creation and resurrection is expressed in the prayers that begin the day. The prayers that follow are the hours of Jesus' last day. By praying this set of prayers in a single day the medieval Christian lived and worked throughout the day in praise of creation and redemption. Here, for example, is a brief outline of the prayers said throughout the day:

Matins: Prayer on rising.
Lauds: Praise at the beginning of the day.
Prime: The wounded Jesus before Pilate.
Terce: The crowds rail on Jesus.
Sext: Jesus is nailed to the cross.
None: Jesus is pierced in his side by a sword.
Vespers: Jesus is taken down from the cross.
Compline: Jesus is entombed. He will rise in the morning.
Matins and Lauds: The cycle of creation and redemption begins again upon rising.

There is a unique and gloriously Christian rhythm to this fifteenth-century spirituality. Time is not mere secular time. Rather, time is defined by the God who acts to create and to enter savingly our historical time and space to rescue a fallen creation. This spiritual marking of time is a powerful antidote to the secularization of life into a meaningless passage of hours. Through daily prayer, time is lifted up into God's time, and the devout are made continually mindful of God's purposes in history.

Contemporary Adaptation

I am convinced that the *Book of Hours* is much needed in our world today. We certainly need the message of the book—that life is given meaning by the God who creates and enters our history to redeem, restore, and renew all things. We also need the spiritual ordering and organizing of the *Book of Hours*. These prayers have the power to deepen our spiritual selves through a daily immersion of conscious prayer in the hours of creation by which we were given life, and in the hours of redemption by which we are given new life through incorporation in Jesus. These two themes constitute the spiritual goal of these devotions, a goal that may be accomplished in three ways of prayer, or in a combination of the three ways of prayer throughout the year.

Three Ways of Praying the Hours

Three ways of praying the Hours are as follows:
A one-day retreat
A weekly cycle
A monthly cycle

Let me explain each of these ways.

A One-Day Retreat

The most powerful way to experience the spiritual impact of the *Hours* is to set aside a full day for prayer and contemplation. Go to a quiet place—a church, a monastery, the country, or a place you have set aside in your home—and follow this schedule:

4:00 A.M.	Matins
5:00 A.M.	Lauds
6:00 A.M.	Prime
9:00 A.M.	Terce

Noon	Sext
3:00 P.M.	None
6:00 P.M.	Vespers
9:00 P.M.	Compline

The Weekly Cycle

A second powerful way to experience life through creation and redemption is to pray the *Hours* spread over a full week. You can accomplish this by following the schedule below:

Sunday	Matins
Monday	Lauds
Tuesday	Prime
Wednesday	Terce
Thursday	Sext
Friday	None
Saturday	Vespers and Compline

A Thirty-Day Cycle

A third way to be formed by the cycle of prayerful praise of creation and redemption is to follow the thirty-day cycle of the Hours. In the margin on the right side of the Prymer I have indicated the division of the thirty days.

The Combination Cycle

For those who wish to do a combination retreat, weekly cycle, and thirty-day cycle, I suggest the following:

Advent:	Weekly cycle plus a one-day retreat
Christmas:	Weekly cycle
Epiphany:	Weekly cycle
Lent:	Weekly cycle plus a one-day retreat
Holy Week:	Weekly cycle plus a one-day retreat on Holy Saturday
Easter:	Weekly cycle
Pentecost to Advent:	Thirty-day cycle

Additional Prayers

The medieval *Prymer* also included additional prayers such as the seven Psalms, the Psalms of the Passion, the Litany, and the fifteen Psalms. Each of these sets of prayers has its own history of development and use. These additional prayers may be used as follows:

Advent:	The Seven Psalms
Lent:	The Psalms of the Passion
All Saints' Day:	The Litany (may also be used during Lent)
Easter:	The Fifteen Psalms

Directions on how to use these psalms during the different seasons have been included in the text.

Conclusion

As you pray, do not hurry. If you need more time than has been allotted, take it! Ruminate on God's word and let it take up residence within you, and let it shape your day-to-day walk with God as it did for thousands of devout Christians in the medieval era.

Morning Prayer

(MATINS)

Matins, meaning "morning," is a set of prayers said on rising. The roots of *Matins* are traceable to our Jewish heritage and to Hippolytus who, in the third century, wrote: "Rise about cockcrow, and pray. For at that hour, as the cock crew [Christ was denied]."

In *Matins* your prayer will focus on the praise of God for both God's act of creation and his act of re-creation in Christ. Begin your day with an interior rumination on Jesus, the very Son of God. Ponder the message that the creator of the world is the one who came to redeem us, yet was rejected. As St. John said, "He came unto his own, and his own received him not" (John 1:11).

Pray that you will be open to receive Jesus Christ, to let him into your heart first thing in the morning and to keep him in your heart all day long. Pray each sentence and word of *Matins* until it takes up residence within you, so that Christ the creator and redeemer is present in all your thoughts and deeds throughout the day.

While *Matins* is meant for early morning prayer, it is acceptable to pray *Matins* at any time of the day. Suggestions have been made on how to break *Matins* into shorter times of prayer for deeper *ruminato.*

- *Retreat:* When you are praying the daily hours in a one-day retreat setting, pray *Matins* at 4:00 A.M.
- *Weekly Cycle:* When you are following a weekly cycle, pray *Matins* on Sunday.
- *Thirty-Day Cycle:* When you are praying the thirty-day cycle, follow the designated days in the right-hand column of the text. Begin with *Lord, open my lips* (page 8), then go to the prayers for the day, and end your time of prayer with *We praise you, Lord* (pages 15–16).

Lord, open my lips

Lord, open my lips!
And my mouth will shout out your praise.
God, come to my help!
Lord, hurry to help me!
Glory to the Father, to the Son, and to the
Holy Spirit!
As it was in the beginning, it is now and will
be forever. Amen!

> Alleluia! Praise the Lord!
> Hail, Mary, full of grace! The Lord is
> with you.

Come, let us rejoice

O come, let us praise the Lord with joy; let
us sing joyfully to God our savior.
Let us come before God's presence with
thanksgiving, and make a joyful noise with
psalms.
For the Lord is a great God, and a great
King above all Gods.
For in God's hand are all the ends of the
earth; even the heights of the mountains are
God's.
For the sea is his. He made it, and his hands
formed the dry land.
Come let us adore him and fall down, and
weep before the Lord who made us.
For he is the Lord our God, and we are the
people of his pasture and the sheep of his
hand.
Today when you hear his voice, don't harden
your hearts.
Remember how Israel tempted me in the
wilderness: They tempted me to prove myself
even though they saw what I did for them.
For forty years I was offended with that generation, and I said, "Their hearts are not
with me."

Domine, labia mea aperies

Opening prayer of praise. When we come before God, our first act of devotion is to be a person of praise. When you are following the thirty-day cycle of prayer, begin each day of Matins with this prayer.

Day One
Venite, exultemus

We are invited to adore and serve God, to hear God's voice, and to never turn away from his presence in our lives.

Even though I am continually present among them, doing things for them, they don't acknowledge me; so I swore in my hurt, "I will not let them enter the promised land." (Psalm 95)

Hail, Mary, full of grace! The Lord is with you.

Glory to the Father, to the Son, and to the Holy Spirit!

As it was in the beginning, it is now and will be forever. Amen!

The Lord is with you.

Hail, Mary, full of grace! The Lord is with you.

Hymn: Whom the earth

The womb of Mary bore him whom the heavens cannot contain.

See the earth, the waters, and all the heavens worship, bow down, and proclaim him.

He is the one who governs the world. Yet he entered the womb of a woman and was contained by her, even though the sun, the moon, and all things serve him forever.

Mary's womb was full of the grace of the heavens.

Blessed mother, by God's gift, the One who is the highest of all powers, the One who holds the world in his hand, was cloistered in your womb.

You are blessed and full of the Holy Spirit by the messenger who came from heaven; in your womb, he who is desired by all people was brought forth.

Glory to you, Lord, who were born of a woman!

With the Father and the Holy Spirit, you dwell forever.

Amen!

Hymnus: Quem Terra

Glory to God who cannot be contained by all creation, yet chose to be cloistered in the womb of Mary.

Lord, our Lord

Lord, our Lord, how admirable is your name in the whole earth! For your magnificence is elevated above the heavens.

Out of the mouths of infants and of sucklings you have perfected praise, because of your enemies, that you may destroy the enemy and the avenger.

I see your heavens, the works of your fingers, the moon and the stars that you called into being.

What are we that you care about us? Why did you become one of us?

You made us a little less than the angels, but you have crowned us with glory and honor, and you have put us over the work of your hands.

You have put everything under our feet: all sheep and oxen, even the beasts of the fields, the birds of the air, and the fish of the sea that swim through the paths of the sea.

Lord, our Lord, how admirable is your name in all the earth! (Psalm 8)

The heavens display

The heavens display the glory of God, and the vault of the sky declares the work of God's hands.

The light of day is God's speech, and the night displays God's knowledge.

There is no speech or language in which the voice of God is not heard.

The sound of heaven has gone forth into all the earth, and the words of the heavens travel all over the world.

God shows his reality in the sun; the sun is like a bridegroom coming out of his bridal chamber:

It is full of joy, and it spreads over all the heavens.

Domine, Dominus, noster quem

God's works are wonderful. Humanity is exalted, particularly because of the incarnation, through which God became one of us and has been exalted as the ruler of all God's creation.

Day Two
Cæli enarrant

God is known to us in the glory of creation and in the wisdom of the Ten Commandments.

The law of the Lord is perfect, converting souls; the testimony of the Lord is faithful, giving wisdom to little ones.

The Lord's acts of justice are right, rejoicing hearts; the Lord's commandment is lightsome, enlightening the eyes.

The fear of the Lord is holy, enduring forever and ever; the Lord's judgments are true, justified in themselves—

more to be desired than gold and many precious stones, and sweeter than honey and the honeycomb.

Lord, your servant keeps the law, and in keeping it has discovered a great reward.

Who can understand his own sins? From my secret sins, cleanse me, Lord,

and from the sins of others, spare me.

If they have no dominion over me, then I will be without spot, and I will be cleansed from the greatest sin.

Let the words of my mouth always please you, and may the meditation of my heart always be present to you;

for you, Lord, are my helper and my redeemer. (Psalm 19)

Glory to the Father, to the Son, and to the Holy Spirit!

As it was in the beginning, it is now, and will be forever. Amen!

The earth is the Lord's

The earth is the Lord's, and everything in it— the world and all who live in it.

For you founded it out of the seas, and you created it by the rivers.

Who will go up to the place where you dwell, Lord? Who is able to stand in the holy place where you are?

Domini est terra

Who is it that will ascend to the heavens? It is Christ, who has triumphed over evil. Open the gates of your heart and let him in.

Only those who have innocent hands and are clean of heart, those who are not consumed by vain conceit, those who don't act deceitfully with their neighbors:
These will receive a blessing from the Lord, and mercy from God their Savior.
These are the generation of those who seek God; they seek the face of the God of Jacob.
Lift up the gates of the city, lift up the eternal gates, and the King of Glory will enter in.
Who is this King of Glory? The Lord, who is strong and mighty, the Lord, who overcomes all evil.
Lift up those gates, all of you; open the gates of your heart, and the King of Glory will rush in.
Who is this King of Glory? The Lord God Almighty, the King of the universe—he is the King of Glory. (Psalm 24)
Glory to the Father, to the Son, and to the Holy Spirit!
As it was in the beginning, it is now, and will be forever. Amen!

Anthem: You are blessed

You are blessed among women and
the fruit of your womb is blessed.
Holy is the mother of God, ever virgin Mary.
Pray for us to the Lord our God!

Our Father

Our Father,
who are in heaven,
hallowed be your name.
Your kingdom come,
your will be done on earth
as it is in heaven.
Give us this day
our daily bread, and
forgive us our sins as we

Antem: Benedicta tu

God was made present in the world through the womb of the Virgin Mary.

Pater Noster

forgive those who sin
against us.
And do not lead us into temptation,
but deliver us from evil. Amen.

Hail, Mary

Hail, Mary, full of grace: our Lord is with you.
Blessed are you among all women,
and may the fruit of your womb, Jesus, be
blessed. Amen.

Prayer 1: Holy Mary, virgin

Holy Mary, you are the
woman of all women, you are the
mother and daughter of the King of Kings.
May we have with you,
the mother of the heavenly kingdom
and of all God's chosen,
a reign with your Son that lasts forever.
V. Holy mother without sin,
him whom the heavens cannot contain,
you bore in your womb.
R. May you be blessed among women, and
may the fruit of your womb be blessed.
[Repeat] - For him whom the heavens cannot
contain, you bore in your womb.
V. The Lord commands us to bless you.
R. Pray for us! Mary, you
meek and humble woman.

Prayer 2: Holy Mary of devout women

Holy Mary,
meekest of all meek women,
pray for us.
Holiest of all holy women,
take our prayers to Jesus,
who for us and for our salvation from all
evil, was born and reigns above the heavens;
for by his love our sins are forgiven.

Day Three

Orisun I: Sancta Maria Virgo

In the *Prymer* of the fifteenth
century, a Scripture reading was
read at this point of the prayer.
It was followed by the prayer
Holy Mary, Virgin, praising her
for bearing God in her womb.

Orisun II: Sancta Maria, piarum

Lord have mercy on us.
Thanks be to God.
V. Blessed are you, mother Mary;
you bore our Lord,
you gave birth to him,
the maker of the world,
the One who made even you!
You are blessed among women forever!
R. Hail, Mary, full of grace,
our Lord is with you;
you gave birth to the maker of the world,
for you bore in your womb the One who
made even you;
[Repeat] You are blessed among women
forever.
V. The Lord commands us to bless you.
R. Holy mother of God, help us!

Prayer 3: Holy mother of God

Holy mother of God,
you deserved to conceive him
whom all the world could not hold.
Because of your submission to God's will,
our guilt has been washed away,
and we have attained
the Holy Spirit
and the hope of endless life,
and will dwell with the Son
forever and ever!
Christ, have mercy on us!
Thanks be to God!
V. Mother Mary,
you are holy and worthy of our praise;
for from you has risen the Son of righteousness, our God, Jesus Christ.
R. We pray for all the people of the world.
We pray for the clergy, and
we pray for all devoted women.
Let those who keep you in mind feel your
help.

Orisun III: Sancta Dei genitrix

In the fifthteenth century a Scripture reading was done here, followed by the prayer *Holy Mother of God*, in praise of her virtue, which enabled her to be the mother of our savior, Jesus Christ.

[**Repeat**] For from you has risen
the Son of righteousness,
our God, Jesus Christ.
Glory to the Father, and to the Son, and
to the Holy Spirit.
He is the Son of righteousness,
our God, Jesus Christ.
Glory to the Father, to the Son,
and to the Holy Spirit!
He is the Son of righteousness,
our Lord, Jesus Christ.

We praise you, Lord

We praise you, God; we acknowledge you to
be the Lord.
All the earth worships you, the Father
everlasting.
To you all angels cry with a loud voice,
the heavens and all the powers and the
cherubim and seraphim continually cry:

Holy, holy, holy, Lord God of creation;
heaven and earth are full of the majesty of
your glory.
The glorious company of the apostles praises
you.
The goodly fellowship of the prophets praises
you.
The noble army of martyrs praises you.
The holy church throughout all the world
acknowledges you,
the Father, of an infinite majesty, and
your adorable, true, and only Son,
and the Holy Spirit who comforts us.

You are the King of glory, Christ.
You are the everlasting Son of the Father.
When you took it upon yourself to deliver us
from all the powers of evil,
you humbled yourself to be born of a Virgin.

Te Deum laudamus

Because everything God has
made praises him at all times,
the *Te Deum* is a blueprint for
our praise. It is a fitting declara-
tion of praise to close Matins.
Let these words of praise beat
in your heart every moment of
the day.

When you overcame the threat of death,
you opened the kingdom of heaven to all
believers.
Now you sit at the right hand of God, in the
glory of the Father.
We believe that you will come to be our
judge.
Therefore we pray to you to help your servants, whom you have redeemed with your
precious blood.
Make us to be numbered with your saints
in glory everlasting.
V. Holy Mother of God, perpetual virgin:
R. Pray for us to the Lord our God.

HERE ENDS MATINS

Morning Praise
(LAUDS)

Lauds, which means "praise," is part of morning prayer. Its use is first described in the sixth-century rule of Benedict. The spiritual goal of *Lauds* is to become the people of praise, for God has called us to be a people of praise. Praise God for everything in your life—both blessings and troubles. The result of a praise-filled life is that we will be full of joy and serve God gladly in all of life.

Ruminate on these passages, and let them enter into your very soul and make you a person of praise. Take your time. Don't rush.

- *Retreat*: When you are praying the daily hours in a one-day retreat setting, pray *Lauds* at 5:00 A.M.
- *Weekly Cycle*: When you are following the weekly cycle of prayer, pray *Lauds* on Monday.
- *Thirty-Day Cycle:* When you are praying the thirty-day cycle of prayer, follow the designated days in the right-hand column of the text. Begin with *God, be my help* (page 18), then go to the prayers for the day, and conclude with the prayers *Lord Jesus Christ* and *Our Father* (page 28).

God, be my help

God, be my help;
hurry to help me!
Glory to the Father, to the Son,
and to the Holy Spirit.
As it was in the beginning, it is
now, and will be forever. Amen.
Alleluia! Praise the Lord!

The Lord reigns

The Lord reigns, he is clothed with majesty:
Indeed! The Lord is clothed with majesty and
is full of strength.
For he has established the world, which will
not be moved.
His throne is prepared from of old: He is
from everlasting.
The oceans roar, Lord: When the oceans
pound the shore we hear their roar.
The oceans lift up their waves,
and with great noise hurl the waters to
shore.
These surges of the sea are mighty,
but mightier is the Lord on high.
Your statutes have become fully confirmed.
Holiness becomes your house, Lord, to the
length of days. (Psalm 93)

Sing joyfully to God

Sing joyfully to God, all the earth: Worship
the Lord with gladness.
Come before his presence with exceedingly
great joy.
Know that the Lord himself is God:
He made us, and not we ourselves.
We are his people and the sheep of his pas-
ture. Go into his gates with praise, into his
courts with hymns, and give glory to him.
Praise his name, for the Lord is sweet: His

Deus in adiutorium

When you are following the thirty-day cycle of prayer, open each day of *Lauds* with *God, be my help.*

Day Four
Dominus regnavit

We become a people of praise when we acknowledge that God rules over the entire creation. We are to view creation as the very works of God that speak to us of his existence and glory.

Jubilate Deo

The psalmist tells us *why* we are a people of praise: "God made us, and not we ourselves."

mercy endures for ever, and his truth to generation and generation. (Psalm 100)

God, my God

God, my God: I watch for you at the break of day.
My soul thirsts for you. For my flesh longs for you!
Just as in a desert land where there is no water, so I come before you; when I see you my lips break forth in praise.
For your mercy is better than anything in life; my lips will praise you.
I will bless you *all* my life, and I will lift up my hands toward you.
Let my soul be filled with you, and my mouth will praise you with joyful lips.
I have remembered you in my bed; I will meditate on you in the morning, because you have been my helper.
And I will rejoice under the protection of your wings. My soul will stay close to you; your right hand will receive me.
My enemies seek my soul in vain: They will be delivered into the hands of the sword; they will go into the lower parts of the earth.
They will be delivered into the hands of the sword, and be like foxes in the hole.
But the king will rejoice in God; all will be praised who swear by him, because the mouth of those who speak wicked things is stopped. (Psalm 63)

Deus, Deus meus
Those who praise God will be filled with joy, but those who neglect the praise of God will go to ruin.

May God have mercy on us

May God have mercy on us, and bless us: May he make the light of his face shine on us; and may he have mercy on us,
that we may know his way on the earth and his salvation in all the nations.

Deus misereatur
We now pray to the God of creation, the One who all people will confess is the true God, and offer him unceasing praise.

Let the nations praise you, God; let all people give praise to you.

Let the nations be glad and rejoice: For you judge all people with justice, and you direct the nations of the earth.

God, let all people praise you; let all people give praise to you, for the earth has yielded its fruit.

May God, our God, bless us. May God bless us, and may every corner of the earth be in awe of him. (Psalm 67)

Glory to the Father, to the Son, and to the Holy Spirit.

As it was in the beginning, it is now, and will be forever. Amen!

All the works of the Lord, bless the Lord

All the works of the Lord, bless the Lord;
   praise him and magnify him for ever.
Angels of the Lord, bless the Lord;
   praise him and magnify him for ever.

Heavens, bless the Lord;
   waters that are above the vault of the sky,
   bless the Lord;
   praise him and magnify him for ever.

Sun and moon, bless the Lord;
   stars of heaven, bless the Lord;
showers and dew, bless the Lord;
   praise him and magnify him for ever.

Winds of God, bless the Lord;
   fire and heat, bless the Lord;
winter and summer, bless the Lord;
   praise him and magnify him for ever.

Day Five
Benedicite, omnia opera Domini, Domino
An invitation to praise the Lord.

The entire cosmos is to bless and praise the Lord: the seasons, the elements, night and day.

Dews and frosts, bless the Lord;
     frosts and cold, bless the Lord;
ice and snow, bless the Lord;
     praise him and magnify him for ever.

Nights and days, bless the Lord;
     light and darkness, bless the Lord;
lightning and clouds, bless the Lord;
     praise him and magnify him for ever.

Let the earth bless the Lord;
     mountains and hills, bless the Lord;
all green things on the earth, bless the Lord;
     praise him and magnify him for ever.

The earth and all its creatures are to bless the Lord: the mountains and hills, the waters, the birds, the animals.

Wells, bless the Lord;
     seas and floods, bless the Lord;
whales and all that move in the waters, bless the Lord;
     praise him and magnify him for ever.

All birds of the air, bless the Lord;
     all beasts and cattle, bless the Lord;
children of men, bless the Lord;
     praise him and magnify him for ever.

People of God, bless the Lord;
     priests of the Lord, bless the Lord;
servants of the Lord, bless the Lord;
     praise him and magnify him for ever.

All the people of the earth are to bless the Lord: all priests, all servants, all righteous, all humble.

Spirits and souls of the righteous, bless the Lord;
     holy and humble men of heart, bless the Lord.
Let us bless the Father, the Son, and the Holy Spirit;
     praise him and magnify him for ever.

Praise the Lord from the heavens

Praise the Lord from the heavens; praise him in the high places.
Praise him, all his angels;
praise him, all his hosts.
Praise him, sun and moon; praise him, all stars and light.
Praise him, heavens of heavens; and let all the waters that are above the heavens praise the name of the Lord.
For he spoke and they were made; he commanded, and they were created.
He has established them for ever, and for ages of ages; he has made a decree, and it will not pass away.
Praise the Lord from the earth: you dragons, and all you who are in the deep part of the earth;
fire, hail, snow, ice, stormy winds, which fulfil his word;
mountains and all hills, fruitful trees and all cedars,
beasts and all cattle, serpents and feathered fowl,
kings of the earth and all people, princes and all judges of the earth,
young men and maidens. Let the old with the younger praise the name of the Lord: For his name alone is exalted.
The praise of him is above heaven and earth, and he has made his people strong.
He honors all his godly ones, the children of Israel, a people who are close to him.
Alleluia. (Psalm 148)

Sing to the Lord

Sing to the Lord a new song;
let his praise be in the assembly of the saints.

Day Six
Laudate Dominum de cælis

The praise of God is not just for those of us endowed with human consciousness, but the work of all God's creatures and all God's creation. God's praise is shouted from the heavens.

Cantate Domino

We use our voices to sing God's praise.

Let Israel rejoice in him who made him, and let the children of Zion be joyful in their king.
Let them praise his name with choirs; let them sing to him with the tambourine and the psaltery.
For the Lord is well pleased with his people, and he will give salvation to the meek.
The saints will rejoice in glory; they will be joyful as they lie in their beds.
The high praises of God will be in their mouth, and two-edged swords in their hands, to execute vengeance on the nations, chastisements among the people:
to bind their kings with fetters, and their nobles with manacles of iron,
to execute on them the judgment that is written. This glory is to all his saints. Alleluia. (Psalm 149)

Praise the Lord in his holy places

Praise the Lord in his holy places; praise him in the heavenly arch of his power.
Praise him for his mighty acts; praise him according to the multitude of his greatness.
Praise him with sound of trumpet; praise him with psaltery and harp.
Praise him with tambourine and choir; praise him with strings and organs.
Praise him on high sounding cymbals; praise him on cymbals of joy. Let every person praise the Lord. Alleluia. (Psalm 150)

Laudate Dominum in sanctus eius
We use instruments to express the praise of God.

Anthem: What a marvelous exchange

What a marvelous exchange!
The maker of us all
took a body with a soul
and was born of a woman,
begotten without the seed of man,
and was made the God-man.

Day Seven
Antem: O admirable!
While we praise God for all his works in creation, the most stunning work of God is that he became one of us in the womb of a woman.

Reading: Virgin Mary, always joyful

Virgin Mary, always joyful,
you were worthy to bear Christ who is
the maker of heaven and earth.
Out of your womb you brought forth
the savior of the world.
Thanks be to God!

Hymn: Glorious Lady

Most joyful of all women, you are above the
stars of heaven, for he who made night and
day was weaned at your holy breast.
Sorrow and sadness are done away with by
the fruit of your womb. The stars have been
made the window to heaven, and you are the
gate to the heavenly being. You are the
dwelling of the king and the great gate of
light, shining bright. The ransomed rejoice
because of the life of a woman.

> Glory to you, Lord, for you were born of
> a woman, with the Father and the Holy
> Spirit, world without end. Amen.

God chose her, and before choosing her
he made her dwell in his tabernacle.

Blessed be the Lord God of Israel

Blessed be the Lord God of Israel, because he
has visited and redeemed his people.
He has established plenty of salvation for us,
in the house of David his servant.
As he spoke by the mouth of his holy
prophets, who are from the beginning,
he saves us from our enemies and from the
hand of all those who hate us.
He has shown mercy to our fathers, and has
remembered his holy agreement.
He swore an oath to Abraham, our father,

Capitulum: Maria Virgo, Semper Lætare

Because Mary bore God in her womb, she is the most joyful of all the people of the world.

Hymnus: O gloriosa Domina

The glory of God that was seen in the tabernacle of the Old Testament, now takes up residence in Mary's womb.

Day Eight
Benedictus Dominus Deus Israel

Because God entered into our history, he is to be blessed forever.

that he would deliver us from the hand of
our enemies so that we may serve him without fear,
in holiness and justice before him, all our
days.
And you, child, will be called the prophet of
the Highest, for you will go before the face
of the Lord to prepare his ways:
to give knowledge of salvation to his people,
and to wash away all their sins.
By God's tender mercy, a light from heaven is
about to break forth.
For God enlightens those who sit in the
darkness and in the shadow of death: He
directs us to walk into the way of peace.
(Luke 1:68–79)

Anthem: Glorious mother of God

Glorious mother of God, ever virgin, you
were worthy to bear the Lord of all Lords!
For you alone bore the King. We beg you to
have mercy on us, and always to pray to
Christ for us that we, helped by your
prayers, may be worthy to come to the kingdom of heaven.

Lord God of all virtues, convert us and
show us your face, and we will be saved.

Prayer: Grant us

Grant us, your servants,
Lord God, we pray, that we may always
rejoice in the health of soul and body.
And we beg you,
by your glorious, everlasting Mother, Mary,
that we may be delivered from the sorrow
we now have and be filled with joy
without end.
By our Lord Jesus Christ,
your Son,

Antem: O gloriosa Dei genitrix

Orisun: Concede nos

Because of creation, and even
more because of incarnation,
we may pray to the God who
cares for our every need.

who lives and reigns with you
in the unity of the Father
and the Holy Spirit, now and forever. Amen.

Anthem: Come, Holy Spirit

Come, Holy Spirit,
fill the hearts of your servants,
and light the fire of love in them.
Send down your Holy Spirit and
we will be made glad,
and you will renew
the face of the earth.

Antem: Veni, Sancte Spiritus

We pray that God's Spirit may come to us and make us glad.

Prayer: God, whose heart

God, you teach our hearts to be true servants
by the power of the Holy Spirit;
grant us to serve you in righteousness by the
same spirit
and to be forever joyful in his holy comfort;
through Christ, our Lord. Amen.

Orisun: Deus, qui corda

By the power of the Holy Spirit, we will serve God joyfully in all of life.

Anthem: Deliver us

Blessed Trinity, deliver us, save us, and
justify us!
Blessed be the name of the Lord!
now and forever.

Antem: Libera nos

Prayer: Almighty, eternal

We beg you, almighty, eternal God, by the
merits of your mother,
the ever virgin Mary, and of all the saints,
that we may be defended
from all adversity—
so that by her prayers we may love and worship you,
by Christ, our Lord. Amen!

Orisun: Omnipotens sempiterne

The entire communion of saints prays for us to be defended from adversity.

Prayer: Of all the saints

We pray to all the saints of God who have
been made citizens of heaven, and we ask
you to pray for us to the Lord.
May we be righteous and full of gladness,
and may we rejoice in our Lord;
may all those who have a righteous heart be
filled with joy.

Prayer: Grant peace

Lord, give us your peace all our days,
for you are our Lord.
Lord, let peace produce virtue in us
and make our lives full.

Prayer: God from whom

God from whom holy desires, rightful counsel,
and just deeds proceed,
grant to your servant peace that the world
may know you, that our hearts may be kept
in your love, and that the dread of our enemies may be taken from us,
so that our times are blessed by your protection.
Through our Lord Jesus Christ, who lives
and reigns with you in all the world.

We bless the Lord!
Thanks be to God!

Wisdom of the Father

The wisdom of the Father who reigns in his
kingdom,
this God-man was taken in the morning by
his own disciples;
he was soon forsaken,
bound, and made to suffer pain, to make
mankind safe.
V. We worship you, Christ, and we bless you,
R. For by your death you have saved the
world.

Orisun: Omnium sanctorum

The entire communion of saints
prays for us to be filled with joy.

Orisun: Da pacem

We pray for God to give us
peace and fill our lives with joy.

Orisun: Deus a quo

We now pray that the peace
God gives us may be given to
the whole world.

Patris sapientia

We acknowledge that peace
comes only from God, who has
saved the world in Jesus Christ.

Prayer: Lord Jesus Christ

Lord Jesus Christ,
Son of the heavenly Father,
by your passion, your cross, and your death,
come between the judgment of our souls,
now and in the hour of our death.
And graciously save all Christians
by your mercy and grace in this life,
and give all who are dead
forgiveness and rest without end.
And to the church give
peace and harmony,
and to us sinful people,
life and glory without end.
For you live and reign, one God, forever.
Amen!
V. By the glorious passion of our Lord Jesus,
R. Bring us to the joy of paradise.

Orisun: Domine Ihesu Christe

The closing prayer points to God's central work in all of history—the life, death and resurrection of his Son—as the hope of the world.

Our Father

Our Father,
who are in heaven,
hallowed be your name.
Your kingdom come,
your will be done on earth
as it is in heaven.
Give us this day
our daily bread, and
forgive us our sins as we
forgive those who sin
against us.
And do not lead us into temptation,
but deliver us from evil. Amen.

Pater noster

We now proclaim our faith and rest in God alone as we close our act of praise with *Our Father*.

HERE ENDS LAUDS

First Hour of the Day

(PRIME, 6 A.M.)

Prime, which means "first," is the initial prayer of what came to be known as the "little prayers." These prayers between the morning and evening prayer (the Great Prayers) sanctify the day by entering into time through the events of the death of Christ. At *Prime* we prayerfully reflect on the wounded Jesus standing before Pilate and his accusers.

- *Retreat*: When you are praying the daily hours in a one-day retreat setting, pray *Prime* at 6:00 A.M.
- *Weekly Cycle*: When you are following a weekly cycle, pray *Prime* on Tuesday.
- *Thirty-Day Cycle*: When you are praying the thirty-day cycle, follow the designated days in the right-hand column of the text. Begin with *God, be my help* (page 30), then go to the prayers for the day, and end your prayer time with the prayers *Lord Jesus Christ* and *Our Father* (pages 34–35).

God, be my help

God, be my help;
hurry to help me!
Glory to the Father, to the Son, and to the
Holy Spirit!
As it was in the beginning, it is now, and will
be forever.
Amen!
Alleluia! Praise the Lord!

Hymn: Come, Creator Spirit

Come, Creator Spirit, visit your servants. Fill
the hearts you have made, full of your grace.
By your mercy, you took the likeness of our
body and were born of an unwed woman.
Mary, full of grace, mother of mercy, defend
us from our enemy, and save us in the hour
of death.

Glory to you, Lord, for you were born of a
woman, with the Father and the Holy Spirit
everlasting. Amen!

God, by your name

Save me, God, by your name, and support
me in your strength.
God, hear my prayer, give ear to the word of
my mouth.
For strangers have risen up against me, and
the mighty have sought after my soul; and
they have not set God before their eyes.
See, God is my helper, and the Lord is the
protector of my soul.
Turn back the evils upon my enemies, and
cut them off by the truth.
I will submit freely to you, and I will give
praise, God, to your name, for you are good.
For you have delivered me out of all trouble,
and my eye has looked down at my enemies.

Deus in adiutorium

Pray every day
Spirituality is characterized by
a "desire" for God.

Day Nine
Hymnus: Veni Creator Spiritus

We must want for ourselves
what God wants for us: a heart
full of God's gracing presence.

Deus in nomine tuo

As the wounded Jesus stood
before Pilate and was con-
demned, so we, too, stand
before our Pilates. As God was
the helper of Jesus, so God will
come to our assistance and
deliver us.

Glory to the Father, to the Son, and to the
Holy Spirit.
As it was in the beginning, it is now, and will
be forever.
Amen!

Praise the Lord

Praise the Lord, all nations; praise him, all
people.
For his mercy on us is confirmed, and the
truth of the Lord remains forever.
(Psalm 117)
Glory to the Father, to the Son, and to the
Holy Spirit.
As it was in the beginning, it is now, and will
be forever.
Amen!

Let us praise the Lord

Give praise to the Lord, for he is good; for
his mercy endures forever.
Let Israel now say that he is good, his mercy
endures forever.
Let the house of Aaron now say, his mercy
endures forever.
Let those who fear the Lord now say, his
mercy endures forever.
In my trouble I called on the Lord; and the
Lord heard me, and rescued me.
The Lord is my helper; I will not fear what
people can do to me.
The Lord is my helper, and I will look in
triumph at my enemies.
It is good to confide in the Lord, rather than
to have confidence in people.
It is good to trust in the Lord, rather than to
trust in princes.
All the nations surrounded me, and in the
name of the Lord I have defeated them.
Surrounding me, they attacked me, and in

Laudate Dominum

Our calling is to praise God at
all times, in every place, and in
all things.

Day Ten
Confitemini Domino

Life for Israel and for us is not
always easy. Life has its chal-
lenges, its difficulties and
troubles. But in the midst of it all,
we are to trust in the goodness
of God and hope in the salvation
he will ultimately bring.

the name of the Lord I have destroyed them.
They surrounded me like bees, and they
burned like fire among thorns; and in the
name of the Lord I was revenged.
Being pushed, I was overturned so that I
might fall; but the Lord supported me.
The Lord is my strength and my praise,
and he has become my salvation.
The voice of rejoicing and of salvation is in
the tents of the righteous.
The strong hand of the Lord is raised in victory; the strong hand of the Lord has exalted
me; the strong hand of the Lord has done
marvelous things!
I will not die, but live, and I will declare the
works of the Lord.
The chastening Lord has chastised me, but he
has not delivered me over to death.
Open for me the gates of justice; I will go
through them, and give praise to the Lord.
This is the gate of the Lord; the just will
enter through it.
I will give glory to you because you have
heard me, and you are my salvation.
The stone which the builders rejected—that
same stone has become the head of the corner.
This is the Lord's doing, and it is wonderful
in our eyes.
This is the day that the Lord has made; let us
be glad and rejoice in it.
Lord, save me; Lord, give good success.
Blessed is the one who comes in the name of
the Lord. The Lord is God, and he has
shined on us. Appoint a solemn day, bring a
sacrifice and put it on the altar.
You are my God, and I will praise you; you
are my God, and I will exalt you. I will
praise you, because you heard me and you
are my salvation.

Praise the Lord, for he is good; for his mercy endures forever. (Psalm 118)

Anthem: What a marvelous exchange

What a marvelous exchange!
The maker of us all
took a body with a soul
and was born of a woman,
begotten without the seed of man,
and was made the God-man.

Reading: In all things I will rest

In all things I will rest, and in the heritage of the Lord I will dwell.
For he made all things to rule me and has put me to rest in my home. Thanks be to God!

V. Hail, Mary, full of grace! The Lord is with you.
R. Hail, Mary, full of grace! The Lord is with you.
V. Blessed are you among women, and blessed is the fruit of your womb.
R. The Lord is with you.
V. Glory to the Father, and to the Son, and to the Holy Spirit.
R. Hail, Mary, full of grace, the Lord is with you.
V. Holy mother of God, ever Virgin Mary:
R. Pray for us to the Lord our God.

Prayer: Grant us

Grant us, your servants,
Lord God, we pray, that we may always rejoice in the health of soul and body.
And we beg you,
by your glorious, everlasting Mother, Mary,
that we may be delivered from the sorrow

Antem: O Admirable

That God became one of us in the incarnation is a witness of how God longs to help us.

Day Eleven
Capitulum: In omnibus requiem

Because God is for us, we can be at rest.

Orisun: Concede nos

At rest, we are now filled with joy.

we now have and be filled with joy
without end.
By our Lord Jesus Christ,
your Son,
who lives and reigns with you
in the unity of the Father
and the Holy Spirit, now and forever. Amen.
Blessed be the Lord!
Thanks be to God!

The First Hour

Jesus, at the first hour, was led to Pilate.
Through false witness he was hatefully
accused and beaten.
His hands were bound;
they spat in his face,
and they swore at him, our Lord,
King of grace.

V. We worship you, Christ, and we bless you:
R. For by your death you have saved the
world.

Prayer: Lord Jesus Christ

Lord Jesus Christ,
Son of the heavenly Father,
by your passion, your cross, and your death,
come between the judgment of our souls,
now and in the hour of our death.
And graciously save all Christians
by your mercy and grace in this life,
and give all who are dead
forgiveness and rest without end.
And to the church give
peace and harmony,
and to us sinful people,
life and glory without end.

Day Twelve
Hora Prima
Take considerable time to
ruminate on the wounded Jesus.
Let your wounds be brought up
into his.

**Orisun: Domine Ihesu
Criste**
We can pray this prayer only
because our Lord was wounded
for us.

For you live and reign, one God, forever.
Amen!
By the glorious passion of our Lord Jesus
Christ, bring us to the joy of paradise.
Amen!

Our Father

Our Father,
who are in heaven,
hallowed be your name.
Your kingdom come,
your will be done on earth
as it is in heaven.
Give us this day
our daily bread, and
forgive us our sins as we
forgive those who sin
against us.
And do not lead us into temptation,
but deliver us from evil. Amen.

Pater noster

We pray *Our Father* and rest in
the confidence that by his
wounds we are healed.

HERE ENDS PRIME

Third Hour of the Day

(TERCE, 9 A.M.)

Terce, which means "third hour," or 9 A.M., is the second of the "little prayers." The "little prayers," said between morning and evening prayer, sanctify the day by entering into time through the events of Jesus' death. At *Terce* we continue to reflect on the suffering of Jesus by recalling the crowds who railed at him all morning.

* *Retreat*: When you are praying the daily hours in a one-day retreat setting, pray *Terce* at 9:00 A.M.
* *Weekly Cycle*: When you are following a weekly cycle, pray *Terce* on Wednesday.
* *Thirty-Day Cycle*: When you are praying the thirty-day cycle, follow the designated days in the right-hand column of the text. Begin with *God, be my help* (page 38), then go to the prayers for the day, and end each day with the prayers *Lord Jesus Christ* and *Our Father* (pages 41–42).

God, be my help

God, be my help;
hurry to help me!
Glory to the Father, to the Son, and to the
Holy Spirit!
As it was in the beginning, it is now, and will
be forever.
Amen!
Alleluia! Praise the Lord!

Hymn: Come, Creator Spirit

Come, Creator Spirit, visit your servants. Fill
the hearts you have made, full of your grace.
By your mercy, you took the likeness of our
body and were born of an unwed woman.
Mary, full of grace, mother of mercy, defend
us from our enemy, and save us in the hour of
death.

Glory to you, Lord, for you were born of a
woman, with the Father and the Holy Spirit
everlasting. Amen!

In my trouble I cried to the Lord

In my trouble I cried to the Lord, and he
heard me.
Lord, deliver my soul from wicked words
and a deceitful tongue.
What will be given to me, or what will be
added to me by a deceitful tongue?
The sharp arrows of the mighty, with coals
that lay waste to my head.
Woe is me, that my stay is prolonged! I have
dwelled among people who do not want
peace; I have spent a great deal of time
among those who hate peace. I am for peace,
but when I speak of peace, they want war.
(Psalm 120)
Glory to the Father, to the Son, and to the
Holy Spirit.

Deus in adiutorium

Pray every day.
We always begin prayer by
throwing ourselves upon God.

Day Thirteen
Hymnus: Veni, Creator Spiritus

In times of trouble, God
defends us and stands by us.

Ad Dominum cum tribularer

God will hear our cry when we
are in trouble. Forsake the
temptation to cry out against
God. Instead, rest in God and
be at peace with your neighbor.

As it was in the beginning, it is now, and will be forever.
Amen!

I have lifted my eyes

I have lifted up my eyes to the mountains; from where will my help come?
My help is from the Lord, who made heaven and earth.
He will not let you stumble; the one who keeps Israel will not sleep.
The Lord is your keeper; the Lord is your protection—he stands right beside you.
The sun will not burn you by day, nor the moon by night.
The Lord will keep you from all evil; the Lord will keep your soul.
May the Lord keep watch over your coming and going, now and forever.
(Psalm 121)
Glory to the Father, to the Son, and to the Holy Spirit.
As it was in the beginning, it is now, and will be forever.
Amen!

Levavi oculos

Our rest in God begins when we affirm that God is in control. God always watches over us and stays beside us.

I rejoiced

I rejoiced at the things that were said to me: We will go into the Lord's house.
Our feet were standing in your courts, Jerusalem,
Jerusalem, which is built as a city, which is a compact community.
For there the pilgrims go up, the tribes of the Lord, to speak of the Lord of Israel, to praise the name of the Lord.
Here are the seats that issue judgments, seats of the house of David.
Pray for the peace of Jerusalem, and for abundance for those who love you.

Lætatus sum

When we allow God to be in control, we can be at peace in our lives.

Let peace be your strength, and may it
abound in the place where you live.
For the sake of my brothers, and of my
neighbors, say, "Peace be with you."
(Psalm 122)
Glory to the Father, to the Son, and to the
Holy Spirit.
As it was in the beginning, it is now, and will
be forever.
Amen!

When he was born

He was wonderfully born of a woman to fulfill holy Scripture. He was made flesh to save
mankind. May God be praised!

Reading: From the beginning

You were from the beginning and before the
world was made.
You will continue, in the world to come, in
holiness and service before him. Thanks be
to God!

V. Holy Mother of God, ever Virgin Mary,
R. Holy Mother of God, ever Virgin Mary:
V. Pray for us to the Lord, our God,
R. Ever Virgin Mary.
V. Glory to the Father, and to the Son,
and to the Holy Spirit.
R. Holy Mother of God, ever Virgin Mary,
V. After childbirth you remained a spotless
virgin.
R. Mother of God, pray for us!

Prayer: Grant us

Grant us, your servants,
Lord God, we pray, that we may always
rejoice
in the health of soul and body.
And we beg you,

Day Fourteen
Antem: Quando natus

The one who saves us from our
troubles is Jesus Christ, who
became one of us.

Capitulum: Ab initio

You can count on Jesus, for he
is from the beginning and will
always be.

Orisun: Concede nos

He will deliver us from our time
of trouble.

by your glorious, everlasting Mother, Mary,
that we may be delivered from the sorrow
we now have
and be filled with joy without end.
By our Lord Jesus Christ,
your Son,
who lives and reigns with you
in the unity of the Father
and the Holy Spirit, now and forever. Amen.
Blessed be the Lord!
Thanks be to God!

Crucify him, they shout

From nine to twelve they bore false
witness and cried with a loud voice,
"Deliver Barabbas to us and put him on
the cross!"
A sharp crown of thorns they placed on
his head, and made him bear his cross to
the place where he was put to death.

Crucifige clamitant

Because of his rejection, he can
identify with us in our rejection.
We can bring all our rejections
up into his, for in his life we find
the meaning of our life.

V. We worship you, Christ, and we bless you.
R. For by your death you have saved the
world.

Prayer: Lord Jesus Christ

Lord Jesus Christ,
Son of the heavenly Father,
by your passion, your cross, and your death,
come between the judgment of our souls,
now and in the hour of our death.
And graciously save all Christians
by your mercy and grace in this life,
and give all who are dead
forgiveness and rest without end.
And to the church give
peace and harmony,
and to us sinful people,

Orisun: Domine Ihesu Criste

Rest in Jesus, from whom
comes peace and harmony.

life and glory without end.
For you live and reign, one God, forever.
Amen!

Our Father

Our Father,
who are in heaven,
hallowed be your name.
Your kingdom come,
your will be done on earth
as it is in heaven.
Give us this day
our daily bread, and
forgive us our sins as we
forgive those who sin
against us.
And do not lead us into temptation,
but deliver us from evil. Amen.

Pater noster

HERE ENDS TERCE

Sixth Hour of the Day
(SEXT, NOON)

Sext, which means "sixth hour," or noon, is the third of the "little prayers" included in the daily prayer. These "little prayers," said between the morning and evening prayers, sanctify the day by entering into time through the events of the death of Christ. At *Sext* we prayerfully reflect on Jesus' being nailed to the cross at noon.

- *Retreat*: When you are praying the daily hours in a one-day retreat setting, pray *Sext* at noon.
- *Weekly Cycle*: When you are following a weekly cycle, pray *Sext* on Thursday.
- *Thirty-Day Cycle*: When you are praying the thirty-day cycle, follow the designated days in the right-hand column of the text. Begin with *God, be my help* (page 44), then go to the prayers for the day, and end each day with the prayers *Lord Jesus Christ* and *Our Father* (pages 47–48)

God, be my help

God, be my help;
hurry to help me!
Glory to the Father, to the Son, and to the
Holy Spirit!
As it was in the beginning, it is now, and will
be forever.
Amen!
Alleluia! Praise the Lord!

Hymn: Come, Creator Spirit

Come, Creator Spirit, visit your servants.
Fill the hearts you have made, full of your
grace.
By your mercy, you took the likeness of our
body and were born of an unwed woman.
Mary, full of grace, mother of mercy, defend
us from our enemy, and save us in the hour
of death.

Glory to you, Lord, for you were born of a
woman, with the Father and the Holy Spirit
everlasting. Amen!

To you I have lifted up my eyes

To you I have lifted up my eyes, you who
dwell in heaven.
See, as the eyes of servants are on the hands
of their masters, as the eyes of the slave girl
are on her mistress, so are our eyes on you.
Have mercy on us, Lord, have mercy on us,
for we have had our fill of those who are full
of contempt, pride, and arrogance!
(Psalm 123)
Glory to the Father, to the Son, and to the
Holy Spirit.
As it was in the beginning, it is now, and will
be forever.
Amen!

Deus in adiutorium

Pray every day.
Spirituality is expressed in our
desire to give glory to God.

Day Fifteen
Hymnus: Veni Creator
Glorify God for the incarnation
of his Son in the womb of Mary.

Ad te levavi oculos meos
We need to lift our eyes to the
heavens and glorify God, who
will have mercy on us.

If the Lord had not been on our side

If the Lord had not been on our side, let Israel now say: If the Lord had not been on our side, when men rose up against us, perhaps they would have swallowed us up alive. When their anger was burning against us, perhaps the waters would have swallowed us up.

Our soul would have passed through a torrent; perhaps our soul would have passed through waters that overwhelmed us.

Blessed be the Lord, who has not given us over to them to be torn apart by their teeth. Our soul has escaped like a sparrow out of the trap of the hunter. The trap is broken, and we are delivered.

Our help is in the name of the Lord, who made heaven and earth. (Psalm 124)

Glory to the Father, to the Son, and to the Holy Spirit.

As it was in the beginning, it is now, and will be forever.

Amen!

Nisi quia dominus

As God has worked in the past to defend his own, so now God works in the present in our lives to protect us from destruction.

Those who trust in the Lord

Those who trust in the Lord will be as Mount Zion; those who dwell in Jerusalem will not be defeated. Just as the mountains surround Jerusalem, so the Lord surrounds his people, now and forever.

For the Lord will not let the wicked rule over the just, so that the just will not embrace wrong doing.

Do good, Lord, to those who are good, to those whose hearts are right with you.

But those who follow after sin, the Lord will take away with the workers of evil. Peace be upon Israel. (Psalm 125)

Day Sixteen
Qui confidunt

Trust in God, turn yourself and all your matters to him, and do not embrace wrongdoing.

Glory to the Father, to the Son, and to the Holy Spirit.
As it was in the beginning, it is now, and will be forever.
Amen!

Anthem: The burning bush

Because of the bush that Moses saw burning, we know that the prayers of the Virgin are always answered. Mother of God, pray for us.

Antem: Rubum quem

There are those who are always praying for us.

Reading: And so in Zion

And so in Zion there was feasting.
In all other cities they rested,
and in Jerusalem my power was demonstrated.
Thanks be to God!
V. After childbearing, you were the woman without stain.
R. After childbearing, you were the woman without stain.
V. Mother of God, pray for us.
R. You are the woman without stain.
V. Glory to the Father, to the Son, and to the Holy Spirit.
R. After childbearing, you were the Mother without stain.
V. You became meek and mild.
R. In you we find pleasure, Holy Mother of God.

Capitulum: Et sicut in Sion

Prayer: Grant Us

Grant us, your servants,
Lord God, we pray, that we may always rejoice
in the health of soul and body.
And we beg you,
by your glorious, everlasting Mother, Mary,

Orisun: Concede nos

God's intent for us is to be filled with peace and joy.

that we may be delivered from the sorrow
we now have
and be filled with joy without end.
By our Lord Jesus Christ,
your Son,
who lives and reigns with you
in the unity of the Father
and the Holy Spirit, now and forever. Amen.
Blessed be the Lord!
Thanks be to God!

The Sixth Hour

At noon our Lord Jesus was nailed to the cross. He hung between two thieves as his body ran with blood. When he became thirsty, they gave him gall to drink. All this pain he suffered: He died for us all.

Hora Sexta
Ruminate on the death of Christ, a death he suffered to set us free from evil.

V. We worship you, Christ, and we bless you.
R. For by your death you have saved the world.

Prayer: Lord Jesus Christ

Lord Jesus Christ,
Son of the heavenly Father,
by your passion, your cross, and your death,
come between the judgment of our souls,
now and in the hour of our death.
And graciously save all Christians
by your mercy and grace in this life,
and give all who are dead
forgiveness and rest without end.
And to the church give
peace and harmony,
and to us sinful people,
life and glory without end.

Orisun: Domine Ihesu Criste.

For you live and reign, one God, forever.
Amen!

Our Father

Our Father,
who are in heaven,
hallowed be your name.
Your kingdom come,
your will be done on earth
as it is in heaven.
Give us this day
our daily bread, and
forgive us our sins as we
forgive those who sin
against us.
And do not lead us into temptation,
but deliver us from evil. Amen.

Pater noster

HERE ENDS SEXT

Ninth Hour of the Day
(NONE, 3 P.M.)

None, which means "ninth hour," is the fourth of the little prayers included in daily prayer. These "little prayers," between the morning and evening prayers, sanctify the day by entering into time through the events of the death of Christ. The ninth hour is the hour of Jesus' death, when a sword pierced his side, and he cried, "It is finished."

- *Retreat*: When you are praying the daily hours in a one-day retreat setting, pray *None* at 3:00 P.M.
- *Weekly Cycle*: When you are following a weekly cycle, pray *None* on Friday.
- *Thirty-Day Cycle*: When you are praying the thirty-day cycle, follow the designated days in the right-hand column of the text. Begin with *God, be my help* (page 50), then go to the prayers for the day, and end with *Lord Jesus Christ* and *Our Father* (pages 53–54).

God, be my help

God, be my help;
hurry to help me!
Glory to the Father, to the Son, and to the
Holy Spirit!
As it was in the beginning, it is now, and will
be forever.
Amen!
Alleluia! Praise the Lord!

Deus in adiutorium
Opening prayer for every day.

Hymn: Come, Creator Spirit

Come, Creator Spirit, visit your servants. Fill
the hearts you have made, full of your grace.
By your mercy, you took the likeness of our
body and were born of an unwed woman.
Mary, full of grace, mother of mercy, defend
us from our enemy, and save us in the hour
of death.

Glory to you, Lord, for you were born of a
woman, with the Father and the Holy Spirit
everlasting. Amen!

Day Seventeen
**Hymnus: Veni Creator
Spiritus**
We can always count on God.
That God is for us is clearly
demonstrated by the
Incarnation.

When the Lord brought back Zion

When the Lord brought back Zion from the
captivity, we were comforted.
Our mouth was filled with laughter, and our
tongue with joy.
The other nations were saying, "The Lord
has done great things for them."
The Lord has done great things for us, and
we are full of joy.
Turn again our captivity, Lord, like a stream
in the desert.
Those who sow in tears will harvest in joy.
When they left Jerusalem, they went and
wept, and cast their seeds.
But returning, they come with joyfulness,
carrying their harvest. (Psalm 126)

In convertendo
The God who is for us, will
restore and redeem us.

Glory to the Father, to the Son, and to the
Holy Spirit.
As it was in the beginning, it is now, and will
be forever.
Amen!

Unless the Lord builds the house

Unless the Lord builds the house, those who
build it labor in vain. Unless the Lord guards
the city, the watchman watches in vain.
It is useless for you to rise before morning
and work until late, only to gain bread.
He it is who gives sleep to his beloved ones.
Children are a gift from the Lord; the fruit of
the womb is the reward of life.
Children are like arrows in the hand of the
warrior.
Happy are those who have many children!
They will not be ashamed when speaking to
their accusers. (Psalm 127)
Glory to the Father, to the Son, and to the
Holy Spirit.
As it was in the beginning, it is now, and will
be forever.
Amen!

Nisi Dominus
ædifcaverit
The God who redeems us will
also build our lives and our
future.

Blessed are all who fear the Lord

Blessed are all who fear the Lord and walk
in his ways.
They will eat from the work of their hands:
They are blessed, for life will be well with
them.
Your wife will be as a fruitful vine, growing
on the sides of your house. Your children
will be as olive plants, around your table.
See, those who fear the Lord will be blessed.
May the Lord bless you out of Zion, and
may you see the good things of Jerusalem all
the days of your life.
And may you see your children's children.

Beati omnes
As we walk in his ways, God
will remain present to us.

Peace upon Israel. (Psalm 128)
Glory to the Father, to the Son, and to the
Holy Spirit.
As it was in the beginning, it is now, and will
be forever.
Amen!

Anthem: The root

The root of Jesse has blossomed. The star of
Jacob has risen. A woman has borne our
Savior. Praise God!

Reading: I have rooted

You have raised up for me a people of worship whose heritage is in God, and my alle-
giance is with the fullness of joy. Thanks be
to God!

V. You are a woman, meek and mild.
R. You are a woman, meek and mild.
V. You are my pleasure, holy mother of God.
R. You are a woman, meek and mild.
V. Glory to the Father, to the Son,
and to the Holy Spirit.
R. You are a woman, meek and mild.
V. Holy Mary, graciously grant that we may
honor you.
R. Save us from our enemies.

Prayer: Grant us

Grant us, your servants,
Lord God, we pray, that we may always
rejoice in the health of soul and body.
And we beg you,
by your glorious, everlasting Mother, Mary,
that we may be delivered from the sorrow
we now have
and be filled with joy without end.
By our Lord Jesus Christ,
your Son,

Day Eighteen
**Antem: Germen ait
radix**

Capitulum: Et radicavi

Orisun: Concede nos

who lives and reigns with you
in the unity of the Father
and the Holy Spirit, now and forever. Amen.
Blessed be the Lord!
Thanks be to God!

The Ninth Hour

At three P.M., our Lord Jesus died. His
death is the great mystery; he cried, "It is
finished," to his Father, and so he gave
up his spirit.
They pierced his side. The day became
night. The earth quaked and the sun
withdrew its light.

V. We worship you, Christ, and we bless
you!
R. For by your death you have saved the
world.

Prayer: Lord Jesus Christ

Lord Jesus Christ,
Son of the heavenly Father,
by your passion, your cross, and your death,
come between the judgment of our souls,
now and in the hour of our death.
And graciously save all Christians
by your mercy and grace in this life,
and give all who are dead
forgiveness and rest without end.
And to the church give
peace and harmony,
and to us sinful people,
life and glory without end.
For you live and reign, one God, forever.
Amen!

Hora Nona
Jesus has died.

Orisun: Domine Ihesu Criste
Closing prayer for every day.

Our Father

Our Father,
who are in heaven,
hallowed be your name.
Your kingdom come,
your will be done on earth
as it is in heaven.
Give us this day
our daily bread, and
forgive us our sins as we
forgive those who sin
against us.
And do not lead us into temptation,
but deliver us from evil. Amen.

Pater noster

HERE ENDS NONE

Prayer at Dusk
(VESPERS)

From its earliest days, the church celebrated both morning and evening hours to signify the pattern of life from birth (in the morning) to death (in the evening). Today as we celebrate morning and evening prayer, we live always in the conscious reality that all of time belongs to God.

The special focus of *Vespers* in the lay persons' *Prymer* is the act of taking Jesus down from the cross. Read and ruminate on each of the psalms and prayers that culminate in the *De cruce deponitur* (he is being taken down from the cross).

Remember that you are "in" Jesus. You died with him, and now you are taken down from the cross. Your sins were nailed to the cross. Take time to reflect on your specific sins that were nailed to the cross. Let them die in Jesus.

- *Retreat*: When you are praying the daily hours in a one-day retreat setting, pray *Vespers* at 6:00 P.M.
- *Weekly Cycle*: When you are following a weekly cycle, pray *Vespers* on Saturday.
- *Thirty-Day Cycle*: When you are praying the thirty-day cycle, follow the designated days in the right-hand column of the text. Begin with *God, be my help* (page 56), then go to the prayers for the day, and end with the prayers *Lord Jesus Christ* and *Our Father* (page 62).

God, be my help

God, be my help;
hurry to help me!
Glory to the Father, to the Son, and to the
Holy Spirit!
As it was in the beginning, it is now, and will
be forever.
Amen!
Alleluia! Praise the Lord!

I rejoiced

I rejoiced at the things that were said to me:
We will go into the Lord's house.
Our feet were standing in your courts,
Jerusalem,
Jerusalem, which is built as a city, which is a
compact community.
For there the pilgrims go up, the tribes of the
Lord, to speak of the Lord of Israel, to praise
the name of the Lord.
Here are the seats that issue judgments, seats
of the house of David.
Pray for the peace of Jerusalem, and for
abundance for those who love you.
Let peace be your strength, and may it
abound in the place where you live.
For the sake of my brothers, and of my
neighbors, say, "Peace be with you."
(Psalm 122)
Glory to the Father, to the Son, and to the
Holy Spirit.
As it was in the beginning, it is now, and will
be forever.
Amen!

Deus in adiutorium

Day Nineteen
Lætatus sum
We are called to pray for the
peace of Jerusalem and for the
entire world. Pray also for an
abundance of food, particularly
for the hungry.

To you I have lifted up my eyes

To you I have lifted up my eyes, you who dwell in heaven.
See, as the eyes of servants are on the hands of their masters, as the eyes of the slave girl are on her mistress, so are our eyes on you.
Have mercy on us, Lord, have mercy on us, for we have had our fill of those who are full of contempt, pride, and arrogance!
(Psalm 123)
Glory to the Father, to the Son, and to the Holy Spirit.
As it was in the beginning, it is now, and will be forever.
Amen!

Ad te levavi oculos meos

In the calamities that come upon us and upon the world, we are not to trust in human ingenuity, but we are to look for God.

If the Lord had not been on our side

If the Lord had not been on our side, let Israel now say: If the Lord had not been on our side, when men rose up against us, perhaps they would have swallowed us up alive. When their anger was burning against us, perhaps the waters would have swallowed us up.
Our soul would have passed through a torrent; perhaps our soul would have passed through waters that overwhelmed us.
Blessed be the Lord, who has not given us over to them to be torn apart by their teeth.
Our soul has escaped like a sparrow out of the trap of the hunter. The trap is broken, and we are delivered.
Our help is in the name of the Lord, who made heaven and earth. (Psalm 124)
Glory to the Father, to the Son, and to the Holy Spirit.
As it was in the beginning, it is now, and will be forever.
Amen!

Nisi quia Dominus

The Lord is on your side. God wants the best for you. In the troubles of life help will come from the Lord, the creator of heaven and earth.

Those who trust in the Lord

Those who trust in the Lord will be as Mount Zion; those who dwell in Jerusalem will not be defeated. Just as the mountains surround Jerusalem, so the Lord surrounds his people, now and forever.

For the Lord will not let the wicked rule over the just, so that the just will not embrace wrong doing.

Do good, Lord, to those who are good, to those whose hearts are right with you.

But those who follow after sin, the Lord will take away with the workers of evil. Peace be upon Israel. (Psalm 125)

Glory to the Father, to the Son, and to the Holy Spirit.

As it was in the beginning, it is now, and will be forever.

Amen!

When the Lord brought back Zion

When the Lord brought back Zion from the captivity, we were comforted.

Our mouth was filled with laughter, and our tongue with joy.

The other nations were saying, "The Lord has done great things for them."

The Lord has done great things for us, and we are full of joy.

Turn again our captivity, Lord, like a stream in the desert.

Those who sow in tears will harvest in joy.

When they left Jerusalem, they went and wept, and cast their seeds.

But returning, they come with joyfulness, carrying their harvest. (Psalm 126)

Glory to the Father, to the Son, and to the Holy Spirit.

Day Twenty
Qui confidunt in Domino

Just as Israel had to learn to trust completely in God, so we, too, must put our confidence in God, knowing that God is for us and will bless us as we walk in his ways.

In convertendo Dominus

Because Israel trusted in God, God brought them out of their captivity and restored them in Jerusalem. God calls us to live in trust and expectancy in the midst of our trials.

As it was in the beginning, it is now, and will be forever.
Amen!

Anthem: After childbearing

After childbearing,
the virgin is without spot.
Mother of God! Pray for us!

Reading: Blessed are you, Virgin

Blessed are you, Virgin Mary,
for you bore our Lord.
You brought forth the maker of the world,
the One who made you,
and you remain a virgin forever.

Prayer: Hail, Mary, the star, Mother of God

Hail, star of David, mother of God.
You, the ever Virgin Mary,
are the gate to heaven.
You received the word "hail" from Gabriel's mouth,
and you set us all at peace.
Exchanging the name of Eve,
You have loosed the bonds of guilty people!
Offering light to the blind,
you do away with our fear
And give us all goodness.
Show us that you are our mother!
Take heed to our prayers.
For us, your Son was born and suffered.
Mary, you alone are the meekest among us all.
Make us free of sin, so that we may be chaste and meek.
Give us cleanness of life.
Make us follow the way of the saints
so we can sing to God
and always be full of joy!

Antem: Post partum

Day Twenty-one
Capitulum: Beata es, Virgo
Mary is always the model of openness to God, a model of trust and readiness to do God's will.

Hymnus: Ave maris stella, Dei mater

Praise to God the Father,
worship to his Son, Christ,
and to the Holy Spirit.
We worship the three in one.
V. Let grace be found on my lips.
R. God has blessed you forever.

My soul magnifies

And Mary said: My soul magnifies the Lord,
and my spirit has rejoiced in God, my Savior,
because he has considered the humility of his
handmaid.
From now on all generations will call me
blessed,
because the mighty One has done great
things for me; holy is his name.
And his mercy is from generation to generation to those who fear him.
He has shown us the might of his arm; he
has scattered the proud and conceited.
He has put down the mighty from their seat
and has exalted the humble.
He has filled the hungry with good things,
and the rich he has sent away empty.
He has received Israel his servant, keeping in
mind his mercy,
as he spoke to our fathers, to Abraham and
to his seed, forever.
(Luke 1:46–55)
Glory to the Father, to the Son, and to the
Holy Spirit.
As it was in the beginning, it is now, and will
be forever. Amen!

Holy Mary, help us

Holy Mary, seek us out in our wretched
condition.
Help the fearful,
refresh the sorrowful,

Day Twenty-two
Magnificat

Because Mary had submitted to
the Lord, her soul was filled
with praise. Like Mary's, our
total submission to the will of
God will result in continual
praise.

Antem: Sancta Maria, succurre

Our submission to God will
make us, like Mary, a people of
prayer.

pray for all the people,
pray for the clergy.
We beg you for all devout women.
V. Lord, show us your mercy!
R. And grant us your help!

Prayer: Grant us

Orisun: Concede nos

Grant us, your servants,
Lord God, we pray, that we may always
rejoice
in the health of soul and body.
And we beg you,
by your glorious, everlasting Mother, Mary,
that we may be delivered from the sorrow
we now have
and be filled with joy without end.
By our Lord Jesus Christ,
your Son,
who lives and reigns with you
in the unity of the Father
and the Holy Spirit, now and forever. Amen.
Blessed be the Lord!
Thanks be to God!

Day Twenty-three
De cruce deponitur

He is being taken down from the Cross

Christ was taken down from the Cross
at eventime.
But the power of the resurrection
was hidden in God's mind.

He is the medicine of life,
for he broke the hold of death.
Look! He is crowned with glory
and has cast down the evil one!

V. We worship you, Christ, and we bless you:
R. For by your death you have saved the
world.

Prayer: Lord Jesus Christ

Lord Jesus Christ,
Son of the heavenly Father,
by your passion, your cross, and your death,
come between the judgment of our souls,
now and in the hour of our death.
And graciously save all Christians
by your mercy and grace in this life,
and give all who are dead
forgiveness and rest without end.
And to the church give
peace and harmony,
and to us sinful people,
life and glory without end.
For you live and reign, one God, forever.
Amen!

By the glorious passion of our Lord Jesus
Christ, bring us to the joy of paradise.

Our Father

Our Father,
who are in heaven,
hallowed be your name.
Your kingdom come,
your will be done on earth
as it is in heaven.
Give us this day
our daily bread, and
forgive us our sins as we
forgive those who sin
against us.
And do not lead us into temptation,
but deliver us from evil. Amen.

Orisun: Domine Ihesu Criste

Pater noster

HERE ENDS VESPERS

Prayer at the End of the Day

(COMPLINE)

The word *Compline* means "complete" in Latin. It completes the prayers of the day, and may be done before you retire to bed.

Regarding the end of the day, Hippolytus wrote, "At that hour all creation is still for a moment to praise the Lord; stars, trees, waters stop for an instant, and all the host of angels (which) ministers to him praises God, with the souls of the righteous, in this hour."

In the medieval *Prymer*, the focus of the *Hora Completorii* (The Hour of Completion) is that his work on the cross is finished. He is entombed. In the morning he will break forth in the resurrection.

Ruminate on your identity with the entombment. How have you died with Jesus? What sins, bad attitudes, cruel statements, and the like need to be buried with Jesus, so that, in the morning when you rise, you will be resurrected to a new life?

- *Retreat*: When you are praying the daily hours in a one-day retreat setting, pray Compline at 9 P.M. or before you retire.
- *Weekly Cycle*: When you are following the weekly cycle, pray Compline on Saturday along with Vespers.
- *Thirty-Day Cycle*: When you are praying the thirty-day cycle, follow the designated days in the right-hand column of the text. Begin with *God, be my help* (page 64), then go to the prayers for the day, ending each day with *Our Father* and *God of the faithful* (page 71).

God, be my help

God, be my help;
hurry to help me!
Glory to the Father, to the Son,
and to the Holy Spirit.
As it was in the beginning, it is
now, and will be forever. Amen.
Alleluia! Praise the Lord!

How long

How long, Lord, will you forget me? How
long will you turn your face away from me?
How long will I endure the pain in my soul,
the sorrow in my heart?
How long will my enemies be exalted over
me?
Consider, and hear me, Lord, my God. Open
my eyes so that I will not sleep in death. I
don't want my enemy to say: I have won!
Those who trouble me will rejoice when I am
destroyed; but I trusted in your mercy.
My heart will rejoice in your salvation; I will
sing to the Lord, who gives me good things:
Yes! I will sing to the name of the Lord, the
most high. (Psalm 13)
Glory to the Father, to the Son, and to the
Holy Spirit.
As it was in the beginning, it is now, and will
be forever. Amen!

Judge me, Lord

Judge me, God, and distinguish my cause
from the nation that is not holy; deliver me
from unjust and deceitful people.
For you, God, are my strength. Why have
you cast me off? And why do I go about,
sorrowful, while my enemy afflicts me?
Send forth your light and your truth: They
have conducted me, and brought me to your
holy hill and to your tabernacle.

Deus in adiutorium

We always begin prayer with
the sense of dependence upon
God.

Day Twenty-four
Usque quo

In the daily cycle of prayer, we
now enter with Jesus into his
entombment. Like Jesus, we cry
out, "How long?" Jesus, who
was entombed for us, knows
our sorrows and our grief.

Iudica me, Deus

Even in the tomb Jesus did not
lose hope in God. In our
entombment we are to praise
God and anticipate God's resurrection for our lives.

And I will go in to the altar of God—to God
who gives joy to my youth.
To you, God, my God, I will give praise on
the harp. Why are you sad, my soul? And
why do you disquiet me?
Hope in God, for I will still give praise to
him, the salvation of my countenance, and
my God. (Psalm 43)
Glory to the Father, to the Son, and to the
Holy Spirit.
As it was in the beginning, it is now, and will
be forever. Amen!

My enemies have fought against me

My enemies have fought against me from my
youth, says Israel.
Yes! They have fought against me from my
youth, but they have not prevailed over me.
The wicked have beat against my back; they
have intensified their aggression.
The Lord, who is just, will stop those sin-
ners.
Let those who hate Zion be ashamed and
turn back.
They will be as grass upon the tops of houses,
which withers before it is plucked up.
They will be like the harvester who has noth-
ing to show, the farmer who has no food.
Those who have passed by have not said,
"The blessing of the Lord be upon you."
But we have blessed you in the name of the
Lord. (Psalm 129)
Glory to the Father, to the Son, and to the
Holy Spirit.
As it was in the beginning, it is now, and will
be forever.
Amen!

Day Twenty-five
Sæpe expugnaverunt
The enemies of Israel have not
been able to defeat God's people. The enemies of Jesus have
not defeated him. The powers
of wickedness that seek to
destroy you cannot! Be at
peace, and bless the Lord.

Lord, my heart is not proud

Lord, my heart is not proud, nor are my eyes seeking evil. Neither have I concerned myself with lofty matters, nor with ideas that are above me.

Lord, I have earnestly sought to be humble and not exalt myself. Just as a child weaned from his mother never forgets her, so I am toward you.

Let Israel hope in the Lord, now and forever. (Psalm 131)

Glory to the Father, to the Son, and to the Holy Spirit.

As it was in the beginning, it is now, and will be forever.

Amen!

Domine, non est

Our position before God, just like that of Israel to Yahweh and Jesus to the Father, is one of humility, an understanding of our place in life.

Anthem: With gladness

With gladness
we hallow the blessed womb
of Mary, that she may
pray for us to our Lord Jesus.

Antem: Cum iucunditate

Mary knew her place and was exalted by God.

Reading: Just as cinnamon

Just as cinnamon
gives off a sweet-smelling scent,
so also is Mary
a sweet-smelling savor.
Thanks be to God!

Capitulum: Sicut cynamomum

Prayer: The unique Virgin

Mary, you are the meekest among all women.
Free us to be chaste and meek like you.
Give us a clean life,
and make us secure
so that we may sing to God
and be glad forever.
Praise to the Father,
to the Son, and to the Holy Spirit.

Day Twenty-six
Orisun: Virgo singularis

Mary's openness to God is a window to our own souls and speaks to us of our need to be open and vulnerable before God.

V. God, go before us.
R. And make us dwell in your presence.

Now, dismiss your servants in peace

Now dismiss your servants in peace, Lord,
according to your word:
Because my eyes have seen your salvation,
which you have prepared before the face of
all peoples.
He is a light to the Gentiles and the glory of
your people, Israel. (Luke 2:29–32).
Glory to the Father, to the Son, and to the
Holy Spirit.
As it was in the beginning, it is now, and will
be forever. Amen!

Anthem: We glorify you

We glorify you, mother of God,
for you bore the Christ.
V. Lord God of all virtues, convert us.
R. Show us your face, and we will be glad.

Prayer: We seek your grace

Lord, we beg you:
Send your grace into our hearts,
so that by the message of the angel
we may know your incarnate Son, Christ,
who was brought to glory by his passion and
resurrection.
For you alone, Jesus Christ, are our Lord.
For you live and reign in the unity of God,
with the Holy Spirit, world without end!
Amen.

Nunc dimittis servum tuum, Domine

Mary's life was fulfilled when
she saw that the Son she bore
was the light of the world.

Antem: Glorificamus te

Day Twenty-seven
Orisun: Gratiam tuam quæsumus

Jesus alone is our Savior. We
trust in him, in his life, death,
and resurrection for our salvation.

The Hour of Compline that closes the services of the day

In the evening
they laid him in a grave—
the noble body of Jesus,
who is the savior of mankind.

With spices he was buried,
to fulfill the holy Scripture.
Then we were saddened by his death—
but in his death, he saved us from hell.

V. We worship you, Christ, and we bless you.
R. For by your death you have saved the world.

Prayer: Lord Jesus Christ

Lord Jesus Christ,
Son of the heavenly Father,
by your passion, your cross, and your death,
come between the judgment of our souls,
now and in the hour of our death.
And graciously save all Christians
by your mercy and grace in this life,
and give all who are dead
forgiveness and rest without end.
And to the church give
peace and harmony,
and to us sinful people,
life and glory without end.
For you live and reign, one God, forever.
Amen!

Hora Completorii

Jesus is entombed. Spend a longer period of time than usual reflecting on Jesus' death. Enter the tomb with Jesus, and ask what you need to bring into death with him.

Orisun: Domine Ihesu Criste

Our Father

Our Father,
who are in heaven,
hallowed be your name.
Your kingdom come,
your will be done on earth
as it is in heaven.
Give us this day
our daily bread, and
forgive us our sins as we
forgive those who sin
against us.
And do not lead us into temptation,
but deliver us from evil. Amen.

Anthem: Hail, Queen

Hail, Queen, mother of mercy.
You are our life, our sweetness, our hope.
Hail to you! We cry.
We are exiled children of Eve.
In you we are victorious,
for you have gone through the valley of
tears.
Turn to us, be merciful to us,
and show us Jesus,
the blessed fruit of your womb.
And open to us the way of heaven,
you who are meek and mild,
you sweet woman, Mary, hail!

Hail Mary, full of grace.
The Lord is with you.
Blessed are you among women,
And blessed is the fruit of your womb,
Jesus. Amen!

Pater noster

Day Twenty-eight

Antem: Salve Regina

We hail Mary, not because she
is the savior, but because she is
the image of openness and sur-
render to God and thus the pro-
totype of salvation for us all.

Prayer: Almighty, eternal One

Almighty, everlasting God,
with the Holy Spirit you are worshiped.
For you were wonderfully made
in the body, blood, and soul of the most
blessed Mother and virgin, Mary,
who was worthy to be the womb of your Son.
Grant that we may be delivered by her prayers
now, and in the hour of sudden death,
and forever. By Christ, our Lord! Amen.

Anthem: Hail, Queen of heaven

Hail, Queen of heaven.
Mother of the king of angels,
Mary, flower of virgins,
the rose and the lily:
Pray to your Son for us,
and help all Christians.
Hail, Mary, full of grace, the Lord is
with you.

Prayer: By the Virgin's merits and prayers

By the merits and prayers of his meek mother,
bless us to be the sons of God,
O Father.

Out of the depths

Out of the depths I have cried to you, Lord:
Lord, hear my voice.
Let your ears be attentive to my cries.
If you remember my sins, Lord,
how can I survive?
But with you there is merciful forgiveness:
So that I may learn from your law,
I have waited on you, Lord. My soul has
placed its hope in you; I long for you.
From the morning watch even until night,
let Israel hope in the Lord.

Day Twenty-nine
Orisun: Omnipotens sempiterne

Because Mary opened her womb to receive Jesus, her openness to God is an eternal prayer for us all.

Antem: Ave Regina cælorum

Mary is the eternal image of our faith and trust in Jesus.

Orisun: Meritis et precibus

Day Thirty
De profundis

As Jesus was laid to rest in death, his last thought was to trust in God. So we, at the end of the day, rest in God knowing that our hope in life is not in self, but in God, who raises his Son from the dead.

Because with the Lord there is mercy, with
him, lavish redemption. He will redeem
Israel from all their sins. (Psalm 130)
Lord, have mercy on us.
Christ, have mercy on us.
Lord, have mercy on us.

Our Father

Pater noster

Our Father, who are in heaven,
hallowed be your name.
Your kingdom come,
your will be done
on earth as it is in heaven.
Forgive us our sins as we
forgive those who sin against us.
V. And do not lead us into temptation,
R. But deliver us from evil.
V. Endless rest give us, Lord.
R. And everlasting life, grant to them.
V. From the gates of hell,
R. Lord, deliver their souls.
V. I believe I will see the goodness of the Lord
R. In the land of the living.
V. Lord, hear my prayer,
R. And let my cry come to you.

Prayer: God of the faithful

Orisun: Fidelium Deus

Lord, you who are the maker and provider
of all the faithful:
Grant us remission and forgiveness of all
our sins.
And may the souls of all the faithful dead
enjoy your forgiveness forever.
By Christ, our Lord! Amen.
V. Rest in Peace.
R. Amen.

In the final prayer of the daily
cycle of prayers, we turn away
from all self-reliance to confess
that God alone is the maker
and provider of all!

HERE END COMPLINE AND
THE HOURS OF THE BLESSED VIRGIN MARY

The Seven Psalms for Advent

The seven psalms are particularly selected to represent the penitential side of Advent. Advent is a kind of joyful sorrow, as opposed to Lent, which is a strict season of penitence. These psalms have been arranged in a seven-day cycle and may be added to your commitment to daily prayer. Ruminate on these psalm prayers and prepare yourself for the wonderful gift of the incarnation—when the God of heaven and earth became one of us to take away our sins and to show us the glory of being human. Each psalm is marked for one day of the week during Advent. Add these readings to your daily prayer time.

Lord, not in your anger

Lord, do not rebuke me in your anger, nor
discipline me in your fierce displeasure.
Have mercy on me, Lord, for I am weak;
heal me, Lord, for I am troubled to my very
bones.
My soul is very troubled: Lord, how long
must I suffer?
Turn to me, Lord, and deliver me from my
trouble; save me, for your mercy's sake.
No one remembers you when he dies; who
will call on you in the place of the dead?
I have wept—every night I wash my bed with
crying; I will water my couch with my tears.
I am troubled because of sorrow; I have
become old because of my enemies.
Depart from me, you workers of evil, for the
Lord has heard the voice of my weeping.
The Lord has heard the cry of my heart; the
Lord has heard my prayer.
Let all my enemies be ashamed and troubled;
let them turn back because of their shame.
(Psalm 6)
Anthem: Lord, convert and deliver my soul,
for there is no one in death who is more
merciful than you.

Blessed are those

Blessed are those whose gross misdeeds are
forgiven, and whose sins are covered.
Blessed is the man to whom the Lord has not
imputed sin, and in whose spirit there is no
phoniness.
Because I was silent my bones grew old; I
cried out all day long.
Day and night your hand weighed heavily on
me: I twisted in anguish as the thorns went
deeper.

The theme of Advent is *waiting*.
We wait for the Lord to deliver
us from our troubles. The Lord
will come. We live in that hope.

The joy of forgiveness

I acknowledged my sin to you, and I did not conceal my injustice.
I said, "I will confess, and tell the Lord of my injustice." And you forgave my worst sin.
Every one who is holy will pray to you for a long time.
And yet in a flood of tears, they will not come near you.
You are my refuge from the trouble that surrounds me: You are my joy! Deliver me from those who won't leave me alone.
Lord, you will give me understanding, and you will instruct me in the way I should go; I will fix my eyes on you.
I will not become like the horse and the mule that have no understanding. With bit and bridle, bind fast my jaw, and bring me near you.
The sinner brings ruin on himself, but the one who hopes in the Lord will be filled with God's mercy.
Be glad in the Lord, and rejoice, all you who have a right heart. (Psalm 32)
Glory to the Father, to the Son, and to the Holy Spirit.
As it was in the beginning, it is now, and will be forever. Amen!

I will guard my ways

I said, "I will guard my ways so as not to sin with my tongue."
I determined not to speak in response to my accuser.
I was quiet and humble, and kept silent; and as a result, my sorrow was renewed.
My heart became hot inside me, and in my quietness a fire began to grow into a flame.
I spoke and said, "Lord, when will this end? How long will this last? Why is this happening to me?

Tuesday of Advent
Dixi, custodiam
In the face of my enemies, I will guard my mouth.

My life will not endure forever; my life feels like nothing before you. Everything seems empty.

I know life is here today and gone tomorrow; we save money and things but don't know why.

So in what do I hope? Is it not in you, Lord? My whole life is yours.

Deliver me from all my sins; don't make me a laughing-stock to others.

I was mute, and I didn't open my mouth, because my punishment is from you.

Remove this sorrow from me. The strength of your hand and your rebukes, has made me faint.

When you correct us for our evil deeds, you make us feel like a spider: Surely life is quick as breath.

Hear my prayer, Lord, and my cries; listen to my tears. Don't be silent, for I am like a stranger to you, and I am only here a short time, as my fathers were.

Forgive me, that I may be refreshed, before I cease to exist." (Psalm 39)

Glory to the Father, to the Son, and to the Holy Spirit.

As it was in the beginning, it is now, and will be forever. Amen!

Have mercy on me, God

Miserere mei, Deus
Make me a person of the "devout life."

Have mercy on me, God, according to your great love. According to the vast number of your tender mercies, blot out my gross injustice.

Wash me clean from my evil deeds, and cleanse me from my sin.

For I know the extent of the evil I have done, and my sin is always before me.

Against you only have I sinned, and I have done evil before you: You are justified in your words, and blameless when you pronounce judgment.

For I was conceived in gross injustice: and my mother conceived me in sin.

For you have loved truth: You have made manifest to me the mysteries of your wisdom.

Sprinkle me with hyssop, and I will be clean: Wash me, and I will be made whiter than snow.

My ears will be filled with joy and gladness, and my bones that have been humbled will rejoice.

Turn your face away from my sins, and blot out all my evil deeds.

Create a clean heart in me, God, and renew a right spirit within me.

Do not send me away from your face, and do not take your holy spirit from me.

Restore to me the joy of your salvation, and strengthen me with a perfect spirit.

I will teach the unjust your ways, and the wicked will be converted to you.

Deliver me from my blood guilt, God, the God of my salvation, and I will proclaim your justice.

Lord, open my lips, and my mouth will declare your praise.

If you wanted me to give sacrifice, I would have given it to you; but you will not delight in burnt offerings.

The true sacrifice to God is a broken spirit; a contrite and humble heart, God, you will not turn away.

Lord, be merciful in your good will with Zion, and let the walls of Jerusalem be built up.

Then you will accept the sacrifice of justice, oblations, and whole burnt offerings; then they will sacrifice again. (Psalm 51)

Glory to the Father, to the Son, and to the
Holy Spirit.
As it was in the beginning, it is now, and will
be forever.
Amen!

Lord, hear my prayer

Lord, hear my prayer, and let my cry come
to you.
Do not turn your face away from me; when I
am in trouble, bend down your ear to me.
Whenever I call upon you, hear me quickly.
For my days vanish like smoke, and my
bones grow dry like fuel for the fire.
I am smitten as grass, and my heart is withered; indeed, I forget to eat my bread.
Because of my constant groaning, my bones
stick to my flesh.
I have become like a pelican in the
wilderness; I am like a night raven stuck in
a house.
I am like a sparrow alone on the housetop.
All the day long my enemies curse me; those
who once praised me now swear at me.
I feel as if I am eating ashes and drinking my
own tears
because of your anger and indignation; once
you lifted me up, but now you throw me
down.
My life has decreased to a mere shadow, and
I am withered like grass.
But you, Lord, endure forever, and you are
remembered by all generations.
Stand up for yourself, Lord, and have mercy
on Zion; it is time to have mercy on us, for
the time is come.
For the stones of Zion have pleased your servants, and they will take pity on its soil.
Then the Gentiles will fear your name, Lord,

Thursday of Advent
Domine, exaudi
Lord, I am in great need of you.

and all the kings of the earth will speak of
your glory.
For the Lord will build up Zion, and he will
be seen in his glory.
He has heard the prayer of the humble, and
he has not turned his back on their prayers.
Let these things be passed down to another
generation, and the people of God will praise
the Lord
because he has looked down from his high
place; from heaven the Lord has looked on
the earth.
He has heard the groans of those who are in
trouble; he has released the children of the
slain,
so that they may declare the name of the
Lord in Zion, and sing his praises in
Jerusalem.
When the people and the kingdoms assemble
together, they will serve the Lord.
He has weakened my strength, and shortened
my days.
Do not call me away to death in the middle
of my life; for you, years go on and on!
In the beginning, Lord, you founded the
earth; the heavens are the works of your
hands.
They will perish, but you remain; everything
will grow old like a garment, like a piece of
clothing that will pass away.
But you are always the same, and your life
will never end.
So let the children of your servants continue,
and let their offspring continue forever.
(Psalm 102)
Glory to the Father, to the Son, and to the
Holy Spirit.
As it was in the beginning, it is now, and will
be forever.
Amen!

Out of the depths

Out of the depths I have cried to you, Lord:
Lord, hear my voice.
Let your ears be attentive to my cries.
If you remember my sins, Lord,
how can I survive?
But with you there is merciful forgiveness:
so that I may learn from your law,
I have waited on you, Lord. My soul has
placed its hope in you; I long for you.
From the morning watch even until night,
let Israel hope in the Lord.
Because with the Lord there is mercy, with
him, lavish redemption. He will redeem
Israel from all their sins. (Psalm 130)
Glory to the Father, to the Son, and to the
Holy Spirit.
As it was in the beginning, it is now, and will
be forever. Amen!

Friday of Advent
De profundis
My cry to you comes from my inner being.

Hear my prayer, Lord

Hear my prayer, Lord. Open your ears to my
prayers; listen to me, because you are faithful!
And please do not judge me: Compared to
you no one can be perfect.
My enemy persecutes me continually; he has
brought me down to the ground. He has
made me live in darkness like those who are
dead, and my spirit is in anguish.
My heart is troubled within me.
I remembered the days of old, I meditated on
all your works, I reflected on all the works of
your hands.
I have stretched out my hands to you; my
soul is like the earth without water.
Hear me quickly, Lord; my spirit is becoming
depressed. Do not turn your face away from
me, or I will be like those who go down into
the pit and die.

Saturday of Advent
Domine, exaudi
Listen to me, Lord.

Let me hear of your love in the morning, for I hope in you. Make it known to me where I should walk, for I have lifted up my soul to you.

Deliver me from my enemies, Lord. I have fled to you.

Teach me to do your will, for you are my God. By your good spirit lead me into the future.

For your name's sake, Lord, you will save me by your justice. You will bring my soul out of trouble,

and in your mercy you will destroy my enemies. And you will cut off all who afflict my soul, for I am your servant. (Psalm 143)

Glory to the Father, to the Son, and to the Holy Spirit.

As it was in the beginning, it is now, and will be forever. Amen!

HERE END THE SEVEN PSALMS

The Psalms of the Passion for Lent

The Psalms of the Passion are particularly appropriate for the season of Lent. This collection from the Psalter is universally agreed upon by Christian tradition as referring to Jesus' Passion. The first psalm, *My God, my God* (page 84), may be said every day along with the intercessions at the end (pages 93-94). The other psalms are arranged for a seven-day cycle. Ruminate on these passages and enter into the passion of Christ; allow his pain to take up residence in your inner life. By doing this, you will experience not only the agony of the passion, but also the wondrous joy of the resurrection.

My God, my God

My God, my God, look at me: Why have you forsaken me? Why are you absent? Why do you ignore me?

My God, I cry every day, but you do not hear me; I cry at night, but it is of no use.

But you dwell in the holy place—the praise of Israel is all around you.

Our ancestors hoped in you; they hoped, and you delivered them.

They cried to you, and you saved them; they trusted in you, and were not disappointed.

But I am a worm; I am scorned, and have become an outcast.

All who see me laugh at me; they sneer at me with their lips and wag their heads around me.

Is this what it means to rely on the Lord? Then let the Lord deliver him, if the Lord delights in him.

For you are the one who brought me out of the womb, and led me to trust in you even when I was nursing at my mother's breast.

I was yours from the womb. From my mother's womb you have been my God:

Don't leave me. For trouble is very near; for there is no one to help me.

Many enemies surround me and have besieged me like a herd of bulls.

They open their mouths against me, like a ravenous and roaring lion.

I am poured out like water, and all my bones are out of joint. My heart has become like wax melting inside me.

My strength is dried up like clay, and my tongue sticks to the roof of my mouth; you have brought me down into the dust and have left me for dead.

My enemies surround me like a pack of dogs; they have closed in on me. They have

Deus, Deus meus

Christ was forsaken on our behalf.

pierced my hands and feet.

I can count the bones of my body; my enemies just stare at me and gloat.

They parted my garments among them, and
they drew lots for my clothing.

But you, Lord, don't stand at a distance from
me! You are my strength.

God, deliver my soul from a violent death;
spare me from these dogs.

Save me from the lion's mouth and from the
horns of these wild beasts.

Then I will declare your name to my brothers
and sisters; I will praise you to all your people.

You who fear the Lord, praise him! All you
descendants of Jacob, glorify him!

Let all of Israel fear him, because he has not
ignored nor despised the cries of the poor.

Neither has he turned away his face from
me, and when I cried to him, he heard me.

I will praise you among the people, I will fulfill my vows in the presence of those who
fear him.

The poor will eat and be filled, and all who
seek the Lord will praise him; their hearts
will be full of joy forever.

All the ends of the earth will remember, and
will be converted to the Lord; all the people
of the world will adore him and bow in his
presence.

For the kingdom is the Lord's, and he will
have dominion over the nations.

All the rich ones of the earth have feasted
and worshiped, and all who are born to die
will fall down and worship him.

Everyone will serve him.

Our children will hear of his wonders, and
the heavens will declare his justice to a people yet to be born; they will hear all about
the Lord. (Psalm 22)

The Lord is my shepherd

Monday of Lent

Dominus regit me

The Lord is my shepherd: I will not need
anything. He has placed me in a green
pasture. He has led me to refreshing waters;
he has converted my soul. He has led me on
the right paths, for his own name's sake.
Even if I walk in the shadow of death, I will
fear no evil, for you are with me. Your rod
and your staff comfort and protect me.
You have prepared a feast for me in the presence of those who afflict me.
You have anointed my head with oil, and my
cup is full of blessings.
Your mercy will follow me all the days of my
life. And I will dwell in the house of the Lord
forever. (Psalm 23)

*Even in the moment of "for-
sakenness," there is confidence.*

The earth is the Lord's

Domini est terra

The earth is the Lord's and everything in it,
the world and those who live in it.
For he has founded it on the seas, and has
prepared it on the rivers.
Who will ascend into the mountain of the
Lord, or who can stand in his holy place?
The innocent in hands, the clean of heart,
those who do not worship idols, those who
do not lie to their neighbor—
these will receive a blessing from the Lord,
and mercy from God our Savior.
This is the generation of those who seek him,
of those who seek the face of the God of
Jacob.
Lift up your gates, princes, and be lifted up,
eternal gates, and the King of Glory will
enter in.
Who is this King of Glory? The Lord, who is
strong and mighty, the Lord who is mighty in
battle.
Lift up your gates, princes, and be lifted up,

*Those who seek the Lord of all
the earth will find mercy.*

eternal gates, and the King of Glory will
enter in.
Who is this King of Glory? The Lord of
hosts, he is the King of Glory. (Psalm 24)

To you, Lord, I have lifted up my soul

Tuesday of Lent
Ad te, Domine, levavi
A prayer for grace, mercy, and
protection.

To you, Lord, I have lifted up my soul.
In you, my God, I put my trust; do not let
me be disgraced.
Neither let my enemies laugh at my defeat:
For no one who trusts in you will ever be
disgraced.
But let all be disgraced who deceive and act
unfairly.
Show me your ways, Lord, and teach me the
paths in which I should walk.
Direct me in your truth, and teach me; for
you are God my Savior, and I have placed
my trust in you at all times.
Remember, Lord, your love and mercy that
are from the beginning of the world.
Do not remember the sins of my youth,
when I lived in rebellion.
According to your mercy remember me, for
your goodness' sake, Lord.
The Lord is sweet and righteous; therefore he
will show sinners the way:
He will teach the humble and show them
his way.
All the ways of the Lord are mercy and
truth; he will lead all who keep his covenant
and live by his decrees.
For your name's sake, Lord, forgive my sin,
for it is great.
Who is the one who fears the Lord? He will
show him the path he has chosen.
He will live in prosperity, and his children
will inherit the land.
The Lord is a rock to those who fear him,

and his covenant will be made known
to them.
My eyes are always focused toward the Lord,
for he will rescue me from my enemy.
Look at me, and have mercy on me; for I am
alone and in trouble.
The troubles of my heart are getting worse:
Deliver me from my pain.
See my abjection and my trouble, and forgive
me all my sins.
Consider how many enemies I have and how
much they hate me unjustly.
Keep my soul, and deliver me; I will not be
disgraced, for I have hoped in you.
My integrity and honesty protect me,
because I have waited on you.
God, deliver Israel from all its troubles.
(Psalm 25)

Vindicate me, Lord

Wednesday of Lent
Judica me, Domine
A prayer to God to be delivered
out of distress.

Vindicate me, Lord, for I have walked in
integrity; I put my trust in you, and have
remained steady.
Prove me, Lord, and try me; test my commit-
ments and my heart.
For your love is always before me, and I
have followed your truth in my life.
I have not taken advice from liars, nor have I
consorted with those who do unjust things.
I have hated the company of those who do
evil; I will not sit with the wicked.
I will wash my hands and declare my innocence, and I will come to your altar, Lord.
I will join the singing of your praise, and I
will tell all your wondrous works.
Lord, I love the beauty of your house, and
the place where your glory dwells.
Don't let my soul be taken away with the
wicked, nor my life be snuffed out with
murderers:

Their hands are dirty with evil doings, and
with their right hand they take bribes.
But as for me, I have walked in innocence, so
redeem me and have mercy on me.
This is where I have planted my feet; among
all the people I will bless you, Lord.
(Psalm 26)

The Lord is my light

Thursday of Lent
Dominus lux meus
Faith and hope in the midst of
stress.

The Lord is my light and my salvation:
Whom will I fear? The Lord is the protector
of my life: Of whom will I be afraid?
When the wicked close in on me to destroy
me, when my enemies attack me, they will
become weak and will fail.
Even when a mighty army rises against me,
my heart will not be afraid. Even if they start
a battle against me, I will be confident.
One thing I have asked of the Lord, and this
will I seek after: that I may live in the house
of the Lord all the days of my life; that I may
delight in the Lord and may meditate in his
temple.
He has hidden me in his place of shelter, and
when evil comes, he will hide me in the
secret place of his shelter.
He has lifted me up on a rock, and now he
has lifted up my head above my enemies. I
have praised his name before the people, and
in his house of meeting I have offered up a
sacrifice of jubilation: I will sing, and recite a
psalm to the Lord.
Lord, listen to my cry to you: Have mercy on
me and hear me.
My heart responds to you; my face has
sought you out. I will still seek your face,
Lord.
Do not turn your face from me; do not turn
me away in anger.
Be my helper, do not forsake me; do not

despise me, God my Savior.

Even if my father and my mother leave me, the Lord will always hold me.

Teach me, Lord, how to live in your way, and guide me in the right path, because my enemies want me to fall.

Do not deliver me over to the will of those who trouble me, for they speak lies against me and prepare to do violence against me.

But I am certain that I will see the good things of the Lord right now, while I am living.

I will wait patiently for the Lord, and be brave and take courage. Yes, I will wait for the Lord. (Psalm 27)

To you will I cry, Lord

Friday of Lent
Ad te, Domine, clamabo
A prayer that God's enemies will not prevail.

To you will I cry, Lord: My God, do not be silent; if you are silent, I will be like those who give up and die.

Listen, Lord, to the voice of my cries when I pray to you, when I lift up my hands toward the holy temple.

Do not let me be drawn away with the wicked, with those who are the workers of gross injustice. They speak peace with their neighbor, but their hearts are full of evil.

Punish them according to their evil, according to the wickedness that lies in their hearts. As they have dealt with others, give it to them: Pay them back.

They have not cared about the Lord's works and the works of his hands; destroy them, and do not restore them.

May the Lord be blessed, for he has heard the voice of my prayers.

The Lord is my helper and my protector; in him my heart has confided, and I have been helped. My flesh has flourished again, and I will give praise to him with my voice.

The Lord protects his people, and gives victory to his anointed king.
Lord, save your people and bless your inheritance; and rule them and exalt them forever. (Psalm 28)

Bring to the Lord

Saturday in Lent
Afferte Domino
Glorify God by remembering his works.

Children of God, bring to the Lord an offering of praise.
Bring to the Lord glory and honor; bring to the Lord glory to his name; adore the Lord in the glory of his holiness.
The voice of the Lord is heard on the sea; the God of majesty has thundered: The Lord thunders over the sea.
The voice of the Lord is powerful; the voice of the Lord is full of magnificence.
The voice of the Lord splits the cedars; the Lord shatters the cedars of Lebanon.
The mountains skip like a calf and leap like young unicorns.
The voice of the Lord strikes like a flame of fire. The voice of the Lord shakes the desert, and the Lord will shake the desert of Kadesh. The voice of the Lord twists the oaks. He strips the forest, and in his temple all shout, "Glory!"
The Lord rules over the flood, and the Lord will reign as king forever. The Lord gives strength to his people; the Lord blesses his people with peace. (Psalm 29)

I will extol you, Lord

Sunday in Lent
Exaltabo te, Domine
Praise to God for deliverance.

I will extol you, Lord, for you have rescued me; you have not allowed my enemies to rejoice over me.
Lord, my God, I cried to you, and you healed me.
Lord, you have brought forth my soul from the grave; you have saved me from those

who go down to death.

Sing to the Lord, all you saints, and give praise to his holy name.

For his fierce displeasure is for a moment, but his favor is forever. Weeping may occur in the evening, but in the morning gladness and joy break forth.

When I had plenty, I said, "I need nothing." Lord, by your favor, you added strength to my beauty. But then you turned your face away from me, and I became troubled.

Lord, I cried to you. I called out to you, saying,

"What profit is there for you if I die? Will my dust praise you or declare your truth?"

The Lord heard and had mercy on me; the Lord became my helper.

You have turned my mourning into joy; you have cut away my sackcloth and clothed me with gladness, so that I may sing to you.

Lord, my God, I will give praise to you forever. (Psalm 30)

Lord, I have hoped in you

Lord, I have hoped in you; let me never be put to shame: Deliver me and do what is right.

Bow down your ear to me; hurry and deliver me. Be to me a rock of safety and a house of refuge, where my enemies cannot reach me.

For you are my strength and my refuge; and for your name's sake you will lead me and nourish me.

You will bring me out of this trap hidden for me by my enemies, for you are my protector. Into your hands I commend my spirit; you have redeemed me, Lord, the God of faithfulness. (Psalm 31:1–5)

In te Domine, speravi
A prayer of confidence and hope.

Intercessions

Mary, unwed and blessed forever,
the vessel made without sin,
the mother of God who has been the temple
of God,
the gate of the kingdom of heaven,
by whom alone God lived in the world:
Bow your ears to hear my unworthy prayers,
and be to me, a sinful wretch,
a helper in all things.
For you yourself were chosen by God
to bear our Lord Jesus Christ
and to be filled with more love than any
other,
to be the Queen of heaven,
and to be our special teacher.
You were made his apostle,
and most clearly the evangelists
were called to be close to God's mother.
Be with me in all things;
be a help to me.
Twice-precious gem of heaven,
Mary and John; twelve godly ones:
Listen to my prayers to God, and he will listen to you.
Drive away the darkness of my wickedness.
For God the Father built a house for his Son,
and confirmed a special privilege
of his love on Mary, the pure maiden.
For when he hung on the tree,
he said to Mary, "Here is your son";
he said to John, "Here is your mother."
For the sweetness of that Holy Love
spoken by God's own mouth,
they were knit together as mother and son.
And though a sinful wretch,
my body and soul have been taken into you
for all time.
Be the keeper of my soul,

Pray this Prayer every day at the end of your Lenten prayers.

and go before God for me,
begging God for me.
And without a doubt the knowledge of your
will is God's will,
and what is not, is not with God.
Therefore, whatever you bid of him,
we ought to receive
by your inherent virtue.
You are a source of such worthiness;
you have given us the health of body and soul.
So, by your glorious prayers call upon
the Holy Spirit to unite us
and to dwell in our hearts.
Cleanse us from all our filth
with the everlasting love of God.
And make us live in the afterlife, and lead us
to the joy of his chosen company of heaven.
For the Holy Spirit lives in one substance
with the Father and the Son;
with him and in him he reigns, God without
end, forever.

HERE END THE PSALMS OF THE PASSION

The Litany for Lent and
All Saints Day

The word "litany" means "a humble prayer for mercy, aid, or special blessing." It is a special form of prayer that goes back to the early church, developing into a more complete form by the seventh century.

It is also a particular kind of prayer: It refers to prayers where a leader proclaims the petition and the congregation responds with a set praise.

This litany is called the *Great Litany* because it is intended for All Saints' Day (November 1).

The *Great Litany* is also prayed during Lent. Make the Litany a regular part of your Lenten devotion. Pray it at least once a week, preferably on Saturdays.

While you pray, ruminate on those you know who have passed into the heavens. Speak of them by name. And remember that you are surrounded by a cloud of witnesses, and that someday you will join with all the saints in heaven.

Anthem: Do not remember

Lord! You are mindful of our guilt;
you know our ways.
Do not remember our sins, for your name's
sake, Lord!
Spare, Lord, spare your people; with your
precious blood you have redeemed the
world.
Do not be angry with us forever.

Lord, have mercy on us!
Christ, have mercy on us!
Lord, have mercy on us!
Christ, hear us!
God, Father in heaven, have mercy on us!
God, by your blood you have redeemed the
world!
God, by your Holy Spirit, have mercy on us!
Holy Trinity, one God, have mercy on us!

Saint Mary:	Pray for us!
Holy Mother of God:	Pray for us!
Holy Virgin of Virgins:	Pray for us!
Saint Michael:	Pray for us!
Saint Gabriel:	Pray for us!
Saint Raphael:	Pray for us!
All holy angels and archangels:	Pray for us!
All the orders of angels:	Pray for us!
Saint John the Baptist:	Pray for us!
All holy patriarchs and prophets:	Pray for us!
Saint Peter:	Pray for us!
Saint Paul:	Pray for us!
Saint Andrew:	Pray for us!
Saint John:	Pray for us!
Saint Philip:	Pray for us!
Saint James:	Pray for us!
Saint Bartholemew:	Pray for us!
Saint Matthew:	Pray for us!

Antem: Ne reminiscaris

Saint Simon:	Pray for us!
Saint Jude:	Pray for us!
Saint Mathias:	Pray for us!
Saint Thomas:	Pray for us!
Saint Bernard:	Pray for us!
Saint Thaddeus:	Pray for us!
Saint Luke:	Pray for us!
Saint Mark:	Pray for us!
All the Holy Apostles and Evangelists:	Pray for us!
All the Holy Disciples of our Lord:	Pray for us!
All the Holy innocents of our Lord:	Pray for us!
Saint Stephen:	Pray for us!
Saint Leon:	Pray for us!
Saint Cletus:	Pray for us!
Saint Clement:	Pray for us!
Saint Cyprian:	Pray for us!
Saint Lawrence:	Pray for us!
Saint Vincent:	Pray for us!
Saint George:	Pray for us!
Saint Fabian:	Pray for us!
Saint Sebastian:	Pray for us!
Saint Cosmas:	Pray for us!
Saint Damian:	Pray for us!
Saint Denis:	Pray for us!
Saint Athanasius and the fellows:	Pray for us!
Saint Thomas:	Pray for us!
Saint Christopher:	Pray for us!
All holy martyrs:	Pray for us!
Saint Silvester:	Pray for us!
Saint Hillary:	Pray for us!
Saint Martin:	Pray for us!
Saint Ambrose:	Pray for us!
Saint Augustine:	Pray for us!
Saint Jerome:	Pray for us
Saint Gregory:	Pray for us!

Saint Nicholas:	Pray for us!
Saint Cuthbert:	Pray for us!
Saint Swithen:	Pray for us!
Saint Benedict:	Pray for us!
Saint Leonard:	Pray for us!
Saint Giles:	Pray for us!
Saint Dustin:	Pray for us!
All holy confessors:	Pray for us!
Saint Mary Magdalene:	Pray for us!
Saint Mary of Egypt:	Pray for us!
Saint Grace:	Pray for us!
Saint Agnes:	Pray for us!
Saint Lucy:	Pray for us!
Saint Katherine:	Pray for us!
Saint Margaret:	Pray for us!
Saint Julian:	Pray for us!
Saint Christine:	Pray for us!
Saint Peronel:	Pray for us!
Saint Radegund:	Pray for us!
Saint Friswide:	Pray for us!
All holy virgins:	Pray for us!
All manner of saints:	Pray for us!
Lord, be good to us:	And spare us.
From all evil:	Lord, deliver us.
From all temptations of the devil:	Lord, deliver us.
From endless damnation:	Lord, deliver us.
From the uncleanness of body and soul:	Lord, deliver us.
From the spirit of lechery:	Lord, deliver us.
From wrath and hate and all evil:	Lord, deliver us.
From unclean thoughts:	Lord, deliver us.
By your incarnation:	Lord, deliver us.
By your passion:	Lord, deliver us.
By your resurrection:	Lord, deliver us.
By your ascension:	Lord, deliver us.
By the grace of your Holy Spirit:	Lord, deliver us.

In the day of doom:	Lord, deliver us.
We sinners pray you to hear us.	
That you may have mercy and pity on us:	We pray you to hear us.
That you may watch over and keep the church:	We pray you to hear us.
That you will give peace to our kings and princes:	We pray you to hear us.
Keep our bishops in the holy religion:	We pray you to hear us.
That you keep all Christian souls from endless damnation:	We pray you to hear us.
Lamb of God, you take away the sin of the world:	Have mercy on us.

Christ hear us.
Lord, have mercy on us.
Christ, have mercy on us.
Lord, have mercy on us.

Our Father

Pater noster

Our Father,
who are in heaven,
hallowed be your name.
Your kingdom come,
your will be done on earth
as it is in heaven.
Give us this day
our daily bread, and
forgive us our sins as we
forgive those who sin
against us.

And do not lead us into temptation,
but deliver us from evil. Amen.

May your mercy come upon us, Lord;
Give us your help.
Be to us, Lord, a source of strength.
Free us from the face of our enemy!
Establish us in virtue and plenty.
Lord God of virtues, convert us,
and show us your face,
and we will be saved.

Prayer: God, whose nature it is

God, whose nature it is
to be merciful to us and to spare us:
Hear our prayers,
and by your mercy and pity
pardon all you have redeemed from their sins.
By Christ, our Lord.
Amen!

Orisun: Deus, cui proprium

Prayer: Your church

Lord, be pleased with the people of your
church, and grant that all errors and adver-
saries may be destroyed. By Christ our Lord.
Amen!

Orisun: Ecclesiis tue

Prayer: Burn with the fire of the Holy Spirit

Lord! We beg you,
let our hearts burn with the fire of the Holy
Spirit,
so that we may serve you with our bodies
and please you with clean hearts.
By Christ, our Lord. Amen.

Orisun: Une, igne Sancti Spiritus

Prayer: Almighty God, who are without end

Almighty God, who are without end,
you are the eternal help of all who trust in you.

Orisun: Omnipotens sempiterne

Hear our prayer for all men and women,
for whom we beg your goodness.
And grant them health of body and soul,
so that when they die,
they might be presented to you in your
assembly.
By Christ our Lord. Amen!

Prayer: Have pity, we beg you, Lord

Have pity, we beg you, Lord,
by your bountiful grace, on all our sins,
and through the prayers
of your glorious and everlasting mother,
Mary, with all the saints.
Keep us, your servants,
and our king,
and all Christian people,
in all holiness.
And may all kindred and people
by prayer be one with us.
Cleanse them of all vices and
endow them with virtues.
Help us and save us.
Put away our enemies.
May we be charitable to all our friends
and all our enemies.
Help all who are sick.
And to all Christians, the living and the
dead,
grant life and endless rest.
By Christ, our Lord. Amen.

Orisun: Pietate tua quæsumus, Domine

HERE ENDS THE LITANY

The Fifteen Psalms for Easter

The history and use of the Fifteen Psalms lies in some obscurity. Apparently their origin lies in the earlier preparation of the priest for Mass, when the Fifteen Psalms were prayed before the service began. Lay people who wanted to imitate the clergy developed their own tradition of saying these prayers before Mass. I suggest these prayers be used during the season of Easter. Pray the first prayer, *In my trouble* (page 104), every day of the season, and then pray the other fourteen prayers in the suggested two-week cycle.

In my trouble I cried to the Lord

In my trouble I cried to the Lord, and he
heard me.
Lord, deliver my soul from wicked words
and a deceitful tongue.
What will be given to me, or what will be
added to me by a deceitful tongue?
The sharp arrows of the mighty, with coals
that lay waste to my head.
Woe is me, that my stay is prolonged! I have
dwelled among people who do not want
peace; I have spent a great deal of time
among those who hate peace. I am for peace,
but when I speak of peace, they want war.
(Psalm 120)
Glory to the Father, to the Son, and to the
Holy Spirit.
As it was in the beginning, it is now, and will
be forever.
Amen!

I have lifted my eyes

I have lifted up my eyes to the mountains;
from where will my help come?
My help is from the Lord, who made heaven
and earth.
He will not let you stumble; the one who
keeps Israel will not sleep.
The Lord is your keeper; the Lord is your
protection—he stands right beside you.
The sun will not burn you by day, nor the
moon by night.
The Lord will keep you from all evil; the
Lord will keep your soul.
May the Lord keep watch over your coming
and going, now and forever.
(Psalm 121)
Glory to the Father, to the Son, and to the
Holy Spirit.

Pray every day
**Ad Dominum cum
tribularer**
Always turn to God in any time
of trouble.

Day One (Monday)
Levavi oculos meus
God is for us, not against us.

As it was in the beginning, it is now, and will be forever.
Amen!

I rejoiced

I rejoiced at the things that were said to me:
We will go into the Lord's house.
Our feet were standing in your courts, Jerusalem,
Jerusalem, which is built as a city, which is a compact community.
For there the pilgrims go up, the tribes of the Lord, to speak of the Lord of Israel, to praise the name of the Lord.
Here are the seats that issue judgments, seats of the house of David.
Pray for the peace of Jerusalem, and for abundance for those who love you.
Let peace be your strength, and may it abound in the place where you live.
For the sake of my brothers, and of my neighbors, say, "Peace be with you."
(Psalm 122)
Glory to the Father, to the Son, and to the Holy Spirit.
As it was in the beginning, it is now, and will be forever.
Amen!

To you I have lifted up my eyes

To you I have lifted up my eyes, you who dwell in heaven.
See, as the eyes of servants are on the hands of their masters, as the eyes of the slave girl are on her mistress, so are our eyes on you.
Have mercy on us, Lord, have mercy on us, for we have had our fill of those who are full of contempt, pride, and arrogance!
(Psalm 123)

Day Two (Tuesday)
Lætatus sum
Because God is for us, we can experience God's peace.

Day Three (Wednesday)
Ad te levavi oculos meos
Keep your eyes on Jesus.

Glory to the Father, to the Son, and to the
Holy Spirit.
As it was in the beginning, it is now, and will
be forever.
Amen!

If the Lord had not been on our side

If the Lord had not been on our side, let
Israel now say: If the Lord had not been on
our side, when men rose up against us, perhaps they would have swallowed us up alive.
When their anger was burning against us,
perhaps the waters would have swallowed
us up.
Our soul would have passed through a
torrent; perhaps our soul would have passed
through waters that overwhelmed us.
Blessed be the Lord, who has not given us
over to them to be torn apart by their teeth.
Our soul has escaped like a sparrow out of
the trap of the hunter. The trap is broken,
and we are delivered.
Our help is in the name of the Lord, who
made heaven and earth. (Psalm 124)
Glory to the Father, to the Son, and to the
Holy Spirit.
As it was in the beginning, it is now, and will
be forever.
Amen!

Those who trust in the Lord

Those who trust in the Lord will be as
Mount Zion; those who dwell in Jerusalem
will not be defeated. Just as the mountains
surround Jerusalem, so the Lord surrounds
his people, now and forever.
For the Lord will not let the wicked rule over
the just, so that the just will not embrace
wrong doing.

Day Four (Thursday)
Nisi quia Dominus
Only God can help us.

Day Five (Friday)
**Qui confidunt in
Domino**
Trust is the key to a relationship
with God.

Do good, Lord, to those who are good, to those whose hearts are right with you.
But those who follow after sin, the Lord will take away with the workers of evil. Peace be upon Israel. (Psalm 125)
Glory to the Father, to the Son, and to the Holy Spirit.
As it was in the beginning, it is now, and will be forever.
Amen!

When the Lord brought back Zion

Day Six (Saturday)
In convertendo Dominus
God fulfills his promises.

When the Lord brought back Zion from the captivity, we were comforted.
Our mouth was filled with laughter, and our tongue with joy.
The other nations were saying, "The Lord has done great things for them."
The Lord has done great things for us, and we are full of joy.
Turn again our captivity, Lord, like a stream in the desert.
Those who sow in tears will harvest in joy.
When they left Jerusalem, they went and wept, and cast their seeds.
But returning, they come with joyfulness, carrying their harvest. (Psalm 126)
Glory to the Father, to the Son, and to the Holy Spirit.
As it was in the beginning, it is now, and will be forever.
Amen!

Unless the Lord builds the house

Day Seven (Sunday)
Nisi Dominus ædificaverit
Only what God builds in our lives will last.

Unless the Lord builds the house, those who build it labor in vain. Unless the Lord guards the city, the watchman watches in vain.
It is useless for you to rise before morning and work until late, only to gain bread.
He it is who gives sleep to his beloved ones.

Children are a gift from the Lord; the fruit of the womb is the reward of life.

Children are like arrows in the hand of the warrior.

Happy are those who have many children! They will not be ashamed when speaking to their accusers. (Psalm 127)

Glory to the Father, to the Son, and to the Holy Spirit.

As it was in the beginning, it is now, and will be forever.

Amen!

Blessed are all who fear the Lord

Day Eight
Beati omnes qui
Fear the Lord and do right.

Blessed are all who fear the Lord and walk in his ways.

They will eat from the work of their hands: They are blessed, for life will be well with them.

Your wife will be as a fruitful vine, growing on the sides of your house. Your children will be as olive plants, around your table.

See, those who fear the Lord will be blessed.

May the Lord bless you out of Zion, and may you see the good things of Jerusalem all the days of your life.

And may you see your children's children. Peace upon Israel. (Psalm 128)

Glory to the Father, to the Son, and to the Holy Spirit.

As it was in the beginning, it is now, and will be forever.

Amen!

My enemies have fought against me

Day Nine
Sæpe expugnaverunt
The wicked will not prevail.

My enemies have fought against me from my youth, says Israel.

Yes! They have fought against me from my youth, but they have not prevailed over me.

The wicked have beat against my back; they have intensified their aggression.
The Lord, who is just, will stop those sinners.
Let those who hate Zion be ashamed and turn back.
They will be as grass upon the tops of houses, which withers before it is plucked up.
They will be like the harvester who has nothing to show, the farmer who has no food.
Those who have passed by have not said, "The blessing of the Lord be upon you."
But we have blessed you in the name of the Lord. (Psalm 129)
Glory to the Father, to the Son, and to the Holy Spirit.
As it was in the beginning, it is now, and will be forever.
Amen!

Out of the depths

Day Ten

De profundis

God's mercy is endless.

Out of the depths I have cried to you, Lord: Lord, hear my voice.
Let your ears be attentive to my cries.
If you remember my sins, Lord, how can I survive?
But with you there is merciful forgiveness: so that I may learn from your law,
I have waited on you, Lord. My soul has placed its hope in you; I long for you.
From the morning watch even until night, let Israel hope in the Lord.
Because with the Lord there is mercy, with him, lavish redemption. He will redeem Israel from all their sins. (Psalm 130)
Glory to the Father, to the Son, and to the Holy Spirit.
As it was in the beginning, it is now, and will be forever. Amen!

Lord, my heart is not proud

Lord, my heart is not proud, nor are my eyes seeking evil. Neither have I concerned myself with lofty matters, nor with ideas that are above me.

Lord, I have earnestly sought to be humble and not exalt myself. Just as a child weaned from his mother never forgets her, so I am toward you.

Let Israel hope in the Lord, now and forever. (Psalm 131)

Glory to the Father, to the Son, and to the Holy Spirit.

As it was in the beginning, it is now, and will be forever.

Amen!

Lord, remember David

Lord, remember David and all the hardships he endured.

He swore an oath to the Lord and made a vow to the Mighty One of Jacob: I will not enter my house or go to my bed—I will not allow my eyes to sleep, my eyelids will not close, until I find a place for the Lord, a dwelling for the Mighty One of Jacob.

We heard it in Ephrathah, we came upon it in the fields of Jaar: Let us go to where he lives; let us worship at his footstool.

Rise up, Lord, and come to your resting place, you and the ark of your might.

May your priests be clothed with righteousness; may your saints sing for joy.

For the sake of David, your servant, do not reject your anointed one.

The Lord swore an oath to David, a sure oath that he will not revoke: One of your own descendants I will place on your throne—

Day Eleven
Domine non est
Walk humbly before the Lord.

Day Twelve
Memento, Domine, David
God is a living reality.

if your sons keep my covenant and the
statutes I teach them.
Then their sons will sit on your throne forever
and ever.
For the Lord has chosen Zion, he has desired
it for his dwelling:
This is my resting place for ever and ever;
here I will sit enthroned, for I have desired it.
I will bless her with abundant provisions; I
will satisfy her poor with food.
I will clothe her priests with salvation, and
her saints will sing for joy forever.
Here I will make a horn grow for David and
set up a lamp for my anointed one.
I will clothe his enemies with shame, but the
crown on his head will be resplendent.
(Psalm 132)
Glory to the Father, to the Son, and to the
Holy Spirit.
As it was in the beginning, it is now, and will
be forever.
Amen!

See, how good

Day Thirteen
Ecce, quam bonum
The fellowship of God's people
is an unsurpassed joy.

See, how good and how pleasant it is for a
family to dwell together in unity:
This unity is like the precious ointment on
the head, that ran down Aaron's beard to the
skirt of his garment;
like the dew of Hermon, which descends on
Mount Zion. For there the Lord has com-
manded blessing, and life forever.
(Psalm 133)
Glory to the Father, to the Son, and to the
Holy Spirit.
As it was in the beginning, it is now, and will
be forever.
Amen!

Now bless the Lord

Now bless the Lord, all servants of the Lord who stand in the house of the Lord, in the courts of the house of our God!
During the night, lift up your hands to the holy places, and bless the Lord.
May the Lord of Zion bless you, the One who created heaven and earth. (Psalm 134)
Glory to the Father, to the Son, and to the Holy Spirit.
As it was in the beginning, it is now, and will be forever.
Amen!

Day Fourteen
Ecce nunc

Bless God, always, everywhere, and in all things.

HERE END THE FIFTEEN PSALMS

PRAYERS AND READINGS FOR

A Time of Grief

The Office of the Dead originated sometime before the seventh century. It was originally used by the clerics alone as the funeral service for the dead. In the fifteenth-century concern for lay spirituality, it was adapted by lay people and used as a way of dealing with the frequent deaths among family, friends, and neighbors.

The Office consists of a group of opening psalms and prayers expressing the fear of death and other calamities. Juxtaposed to the difficulties of life is the constant commitment to praise God in all things.

The entire Office consists of *Dirige;* the First, Second, and Third prayers of mourning (Nocturns); the praise (Lauds); and the concluding praise (Commendations).

Pray this Office when you have lost a loved one or when you have been bruised by an extraordinary life-changing event. These prayers will touch your heart and bring healing to your life.

The Office of the Dead is quite long and constitutes almost a second book. It was said at the funeral in the church, at the grave site, and in private.

In today's world we do not have many options given to us for dealing with grief. The many psalms chosen for the medieval death and burial process are particularly helpful for those who mourn a death or some other calamitous situation. You may wish to stop the daily prayers and turn to the cycle of prayers in the Office of the Dead whenever you go through trying times.

In keeping with the tradition of the fifteenth century, when the use of the *Prymer* was varied, I have suggested three different uses of these prayers. First, you can pray all the prayers in a one-day retreat. Or second, in a week of prayers:

Prayer	*One-Day Retreat*	*One Week*
Dirige	6 A.M.	Monday and Tuesday
First Prayer of mourning	9 A.M.	Wednesday
Second Prayer of mourning	Noon	Thursday
Third Prayer of mourning	3 P.M.	Friday
In Praise	6 P.M.	Saturday
Concluding Praise	9 P.M.	Sunday

Finally, you may choose to spread the prayers over a thirty-day cycle, as outlined on the next page.

As you pray, do not hurry. If you need more time than has been suggested, take it! Ruminate on God's word and let it bring healing to your broken life.

Office of the Dead

(DIRIGE)

The word *Dirige* refers to the funeral and the office of the dead. It begins with a series of psalms and prayers that express the double theme of death and adversity on the one hand, and the praise of God and confidence in his mercy on the other. In these prayers the sadness of death and tribulation is expressed in such a way that the depth of sorrow may find release and be free, even in tribulation, to praise the Almighty.

- *Retreat*: When you are praying these prayers for a time of grief in a one-day retreat setting, pray the Office of the Dead at 6 A.M.
- *Weekly Cycle*: When you are following a weekly cycle, pray the office of the Dead on both Monday and Tuesday.
- *Thirty-Day Cycle*: When you are praying the thirty-day cycle, pray the Office of the Dead every day, and follow the directions for daily prayer located in the right-hand column that begins with the First Prayer of mourning, or Nocturn (page 125).

I have loved the Lord

I have loved the Lord, because he hears my voice in prayer.
Because he has listened to me, I will seek him as long as I live.
I was burdened with trouble and sorrow, and I called on the name of the Lord. Lord, deliver my soul!
The Lord is merciful and just, and our God shows us his mercy.
The Lord protects his children. I was humbled, and he delivered me.
I will turn and find rest in him, for the Lord has been generous to me.
He has delivered my soul from death, my eyes from tears, my feet from falling.
I will please the Lord right now, while I am living. (Psalm 116)
Anthem: I will please the Lord right now, while I am living.

Dilexi quoniam
The prayer of a person in affliction expresses a lively confidence in God.

In my trouble I cried to the Lord

In my trouble I cried to the Lord, and he heard me.
Lord, deliver my soul from liars, and from deceitful people.
What can God give to these deceivers, or what will be added to them?
He will shoot the sharp arrows of the mighty at them, with tips of fire that burn and destroy.
Woe is me, that my journey goes on and on!
I have dwelt with the inhabitants of Kedar.
For too long my soul has traveled with those who hate peace.
When I spoke peace to them, they fought against me without cause. (Psalm 120)
Anthem: Woe is me! For too long my soul has traveled with those who hate peace.

Ad Dominum cum tribularer
A prayer offered in the time of tribulation.

I have lifted my eyes

I have lifted up my eyes to the mountains;
from where will my help come?
My help is from the Lord, who made heaven
and earth.
He will not let you stumble; the One who
keeps Israel will not sleep.
The Lord is your keeper; the Lord is your
protection—he stands right beside you.
The sun will not burn you by day, nor the
moon by night.
The Lord will keep you from all evil; the
Lord will keep your soul.
May the Lord keep watch over your coming
and going, now and forever.
(Psalm 121)
Glory to the Father, to the Son, and to the
Holy Spirit.
As it was in the beginning, it is now, and will
be forever.
Amen!

Levavi oculos
We are called to rest in the
hand of God.

Out of the depths

Out of the depths I have cried to you, Lord:
Lord, hear my voice.
Let your ears be attentive to my cries.
If you remember my sins, Lord,
how can I survive?
But with you there is merciful forgiveness:
so that I may learn from your law,
I have waited on you, Lord. My soul has
placed its hope in you; I long for you.
From the morning watch even until night,
let Israel hope in the Lord.
Because with the Lord there is mercy, with
him, lavish redemption. He will redeem
Israel from all their sins. (Psalm 130)
Anthem: If you remember my sins, Lord,
how can I survive?

De profundis
We offer our prayer to God
from the very depths of our
inner being.

I will praise you

I will praise you, Lord, with my whole heart,
for you have heard the words of my mouth.
I will sing praise to you in the sight of the
angels: I will worship towards your holy
temple,
and I will give glory to your name for your
mercy, and for your truth:
For you have magnified your holy name
above all.
No matter what day I call upon you, hear
me. You will strengthen my soul.
May all the kings of the earth give glory to
you, for they have heard all the words of
your mouth.
And let them sing in the Lord's ways, for the
Lord's glory is great.
For the Lord is high, and looks on the low,
and from on high he sees far off.
If I am in trouble, you will help me: You
have stretched forth your hand against the
wrath of my enemies, and your right hand
has saved me.
The Lord will repay for me; your mercy,
Lord, lasts forever.
Do not despise the works of your hands.
(Psalm 138)
Anthem: Lord, do not despise the works of
your hands.

Confitebor

Even in adversity, we praise
God for all his benefits.

My soul magnifies

And Mary said: My soul magnifies the Lord,
and my spirit has rejoiced in God, my Savior,
because he has considered the humility of his
handmaid.
From now on all generations will call me
blessed,
because the mighty One has done great
things for me; holy is his name.

Magnificat

With Mary, we magnify the
Lord

And his mercy is from generation to generation to those who fear him.
He has shown us the might of his arm; he has scattered the proud and conceited.
He has put down the mighty from their seat and has exalted the humble.
He has filled the hungry with good things, and the rich he has sent away empty.
He has received Israel his servant, keeping in mind his mercy,
as he spoke to our fathers, to Abraham and to his seed, forever.
(Luke 1:46–55)
Anthem: I heard a voice from heaven saying: "Blessed are the dead who die in the Lord."

> From the gates of hell,
> Lord, deliver his/her soul.
> Lord, have mercy on us.
> Christ, have mercy on us.
> Lord, have mercy on us.

Our Father   **Pater noster**

Our Father,
who are in heaven,
hallowed be your name.
Your kingdom come,
your will be done on earth
as it is in heaven.
Give us this day
our daily bread, and
forgive us our sins as we
forgive those who sin
against us.
And do not lead us into temptation,
but deliver us from evil. Amen.

Praise the Lord, my soul

Praise the Lord, my soul.

I will praise the Lord all my life; I will sing to my God as long as I live.

Do not put your trust in princes, in humans who cannot grant salvation.

His spirit will go forth, and he will return into the earth; in that day all their plans will perish.

Blessed are those who have the God of Jacob for their helper, whose hope is in the Lord God, who made heaven and earth, the sea, and all things that are in them;

who keeps truth forever; who executes judgment for those who suffer wrong; who gives food to the hungry.

The Lord lifts up those who are bowed down; the Lord loves the just.

The Lord keeps the strangers. He will support the fatherless and the widow, and he will destroy the ways of sinners.

The Lord will reign forever—your God, Zion, generation after generation.

(Psalm 146)

V. Endless rest, give to him, Lord,

R. And everlasting life.

V. From the gates of hell,

R. Lord, deliver her soul.

V. I will live to see the goodness of the Lord

R. In the land of the living.

V. Lord, hear my prayer,

R. And let my cry come to you.

Lauda, anima mea

Even in adversity we will put our trust in God.

Prayer: Lord, incline your ear

Lord, incline your ear to our prayers with which we plead to you to save the souls of your servants, both men and women, whom you have called to pass out of this world into eternal peace and light,

Orisun: Inclina, Domine

and into the fellowship of heaven.
By Christ, our Lord. Amen!

God, who calls us to respect our father and mother

God, who calls us to respect our father and mother:
Have mercy on the souls
of my father and mother,
and forgive them all their sins.
And may we live with them in endless bliss.
Amen!

Deus, qui patrem et matrem

God, whose nature it is

God, whose nature it is
to have mercy and to spare us,
we pray and beg you
to save the soul of your servant
whom you have called to pass out of this world,
so that he may not be taken into the hands
of our enemies.
Do not forget him,
but take him up with the holy angels,
and lead him into the presence of eternal life
so that he hopes and believes in you.
Let him be forever glad in the company of heaven. Amen!

Deus, cui proprium

God of mercy

God of mercy,
grant to the soul of your servant
whose memory we make today
a time of refreshing,
blissful rest, and
clearness of light.
Amen!

Deus indulgenciarum

First Prayer of Mourning
(NOCTURN)

The first set of prayers in the time of mourning or distress deals with the unfairness of life and the weariness of life in the face of calamity. The reader identifies with Job, who cries, "My soul is weary of life."

- *Retreat*: When you are praying the Prayers for a Time of Grief in a one-day retreat setting, pray this First Prayer at 9 A.M.
- *Weekly Cycle*: When you are following a weekly cycle, pray the First Prayer on Wednesday.
- *Thirty-Day Cycle*: When you are praying the thirty-day cycle, follow the directions for daily prayer located in the right-hand column.

Listen to my words

Listen to my words, Lord; hear my cry.
Consider the voice of my prayer, my King
and my God.
For to you I will pray; Lord, in the morning
you will hear my voice.
You do not take pleasure in evil; the wicked
cannot live with you.
The arrogant cannot come before you; you
will destroy those who lie, for you will not
tolerate deceitful people.
But I, by your mercy, will enter your house,
and will bow before you.
Lead me into your righteousness; guide me
in paths that will lead me away from my
enemies.
I cannot trust the evil ones—their hearts are
filled with malice. They speak with deceit
and hate.
Declare them guilty, Lord! Banish them, for
they have rebelled against you.
Let all who rest in you be glad and sing
for joy.
Protect those who love you; for you surround the righteous with your favor like a
shield. (Psalm 5)
Anthem: My Lord God, prepare my way in
your sight.

Day One
Verba mea
Hope in the Lord! For he has
struck down the evil of death,
and by his resurrection promises
eternal life.

Lord, not in your anger

Lord, do not rebuke me in your anger, nor
discipline me in your fierce displeasure.
Have mercy on me, Lord, for I am weak; heal
me, Lord, for I am troubled to my very bones.
My soul is very troubled: Lord, how long
must I suffer?
Turn to me, Lord, and deliver me from my
trouble; save me, for your mercy's sake.
No one remembers you when he dies; who

**Domine, ne in furore
tuo**
How long, Lord, will it take for
my soul to be healed?

will call on you in the place of the dead?
I have wept—every night I wash my bed with
crying; I will water my couch with my tears.
I am troubled because of sorrow; I have
become old because of my enemies.
Depart from me, you workers of evil, for the
Lord has heard the voice of my weeping.
The Lord has heard the cry of my heart; the
Lord has heard my prayer.
Let all my enemies be ashamed and troubled;
let them turn back because of their shame.
(Psalm 6)
Anthem: Lord, convert and deliver my soul,
for there is no one in death who is more
merciful than you.

Lord, my God, I have put my trust in you

Lord, my God, I have put my trust in you;
save and deliver me from all those who persecute me,
so that when evil ones try to destroy me and
no one can save me, you will be there.
Lord, my God, if I have done this thing, if
there is sin in my hands,
if I have repaid evil to those who paid me
evil, let me deservedly fall empty before my
enemies.
Then let the enemy pursue my soul, and take
it, and tread down my life on the earth, and
bring down my glory to the dust.
Rise up, Lord, in your anger; may you be
exalted before my enemies.
Arise, Lord, my God, in your justice, and a
congregation of people will surround you.
And for their sakes, return on high.
The Lord judges the people. Judge me, Lord,
according to my justice, and according to my
innocence.
The wickedness of sinners will be no more,

Day Two
**Domine, Deus meus!
In te speravi**
I trust you, God. Strengthen my
trust and encourage me to lean
on you day by day.

and you will direct the just: You are the
searcher of hearts and minds.
My help is from the Lord, who saves the
upright of heart.
God is a just judge, strong and patient: Is he
angry every day?
For those who do not turn to him, he will
brandish his sword; he will bend his bow,
and make it ready.
His bow is an instrument of death: He has
made his arrows of fire.
One who is full of injustice and has brought
forth sorrow, brings gross injustice upon
himself.
He has opened a pit and dug it, and he has
fallen into the hole he made.
His sorrow will be turned against him, and
his evil will crush his crown.
I will give glory to the Lord according to his
justice, and will sing to the name of the
Lord, the most high. (Psalm 7)
Anthem: If at any time he comes to take my
soul, make it safe.
V. From the gates of hell,
R. Lord, deliver her soul.

Our Father

Pater noster

Our Father,
who are in heaven,
hallowed be your name.
Your kingdom come,
your will be done on earth
as it is in heaven.
Give us this day
our daily bread, and
forgive us our sins as we
forgive those who sin
against us.
And do not lead us into temptation,
but deliver us from evil. Amen.

Reading I: I have given up hope

I have given up hope. I do not want to live any longer. Spare me, for my days are nothing.

What are humans that you should magnify them? Why do you love them so much that you visit them early in the morning, and you test them without warning?

How long will it be before you spare me, how long will you allow me to suffer?

Have I sinned? What have I done to you, the keeper of humanity?

Why have you opposed me? Have I become burdensome to you?

Why don't you remove my sin, and why don't you take away my wickedness?

I will now sleep in the dust, and if you seek me in the morning, I will be gone.
(Job 7:16–21)

V. I believe that my Savior lives, and that I will rise up on the last day; and in my flesh I will see God, my Savior.

R. I myself will see him, and not another. For my eyes will see him,

[Repeat] And in my flesh I will see God, my Savior.

Day Three
Lectio I
We confess how feeble our hope really is.

Reading II: My soul is weary

My soul is weary of my life; I will complain and speak out of the bitterness within me.

I will say to God, "Do not condemn me. Tell me why you judge me so.

Does it please you to oppress me, the work of your own hands, and to look with favor on the wicked?

Do you have eyes of flesh? Do you see as humans see?

Are your days as the days of humans, and are your years as human years,

Lectio II: Tedet anima mea
I am weary of my pain.

that you should inquire after my evil and search after my sin?
You should know that I have done no wicked thing, whereas there is no human who can deliver out of your hand."
(Job 10:1–7)
V. You raised Lazarus from the dead: Grant him/her rest in that place of forgiveness.
R. You will come to judge the living and the dead, and the world by fire.
[Repeat] Lord, grant him/her rest in that place of forgiveness.

Reading III: Your hands have made me

Your hands have made me and fashioned me. Will you now suddenly destroy me?
Remember, I beg you, that you have made me as the clay, and you will bring me to dust again.
Did you not pour me out like milk, and curdle me like cheese?
You have clothed me with skin and flesh.
You have put me together with bones and sinews.
You have granted me life and mercy, and your visit has preserved my spirit.
(Job 10:8–12)
V. Lord, when you come to judge the earth, where will I hide my face from your fierce anger. For I have sinned much in my life.
R. I hate my sins and I am ashamed before you when you come with judgment; do not condemn me,
[Repeat] For I have sinned much in my life.

Lectio III: Manus tue

Remember, Lord, that you made me. I am yours. Bring hope to my spirit.

Second Prayer of Mourning
(NOCTURN)

The second set of prayers of mourning continues to focus on the plight of the human situation—its shortness, its trouble, its anxieties. But the prayers of the psalms are more hopeful and foresee the pained one turning to praise.

- *Retreat*: When you are praying the Prayers for a Time of Grief in a one-day retreat setting, pray this Second Prayer at noon.
- *Weekly Cycle*: When you are following a weekly cycle, pray the Second Prayer on Thursday.
- *Thirty-Day Cycle*: When you are praying the thirty-day cycle, follow the directions for daily prayer located in the right-hand column.

The Lord is my shepherd

The Lord is my shepherd: I will not need anything. He has placed me in a green pasture. He has led me to refreshing waters; he has converted my soul. He has led me on the right paths, for his own name's sake.

Even if I walk in the shadow of death, I will fear no evil, for you are with me. Your rod and your staff comfort and protect me.

You have prepared a feast for me in the presence of those who afflict me.

You have anointed my head with oil, and my cup is full of blessings.

Your mercy will follow me all the days of my life. And I will dwell in the house of the Lord forever. (Psalm 23)

Anthem: He has placed me in a green pasture.

Day Four

Dominus regit me

Lord, you rule my life. Comfort me in my times of great need.

To you, Lord, I have lifted up my soul

To you, Lord, I have lifted up my soul.

In you, my God, I put my trust; do not let me be disgraced.

Neither let my enemies laugh at my defeat: For no one who trusts in you will ever be disgraced.

But let all be disgraced who deceive and act unfairly.

Show me your ways, Lord, and teach me the paths in which I should walk.

Direct me in your truth, and teach me; for you are God my Savior, and I have placed my trust in you at all times.

Remember, Lord, your love and mercy that are from the beginning of the world.

Do not remember the sins of my youth, when I lived in rebellion.

According to your mercy remember me, for

Ad te Domine levavi

Guide me, Lord, in this time of grief, and deliver me from my pain.

your goodness' sake, Lord.
The Lord is sweet and righteous; therefore he
will show sinners the way:
He will teach the humble and show them his
way.
All the ways of the Lord are mercy and
truth; he will lead all who keep his covenant
and live by his decrees.
For your name's sake, Lord, forgive my sin,
for it is great.
Who is the one who fears the Lord? He will
show him the path he has chosen.
He will live in prosperity, and his children
will inherit the land.
The Lord is a rock to those who fear him,
and his covenant will be made known to
them.
My eyes are always focused toward the Lord,
for he will rescue me from my enemy.
Look at me, and have mercy on me; for I am
alone and in trouble.
The troubles of my heart are getting worse:
Deliver me from my pain.
See my abjection and my trouble, and forgive
me all my sins.
Consider how many enemies I have and how
much they hate me unjustly.
Keep my soul, and deliver me; I will not be
disgraced, for I have hoped in you.
My integrity and honesty protect me,
because I have waited on you.
God, deliver Israel from all its troubles.
(Psalm 25)
Anthem: Lord, do not remember the sins of
my soul and my ignorance.

The Lord is my light
The Lord is my light and my salvation:
Whom will I fear? The Lord is the protector
of my life: Of whom will I be afraid?

Day Five
Dominus illuminatio
Teach me, Lord, to bring my
grief to you and to find rest and
peace in my heart and soul.

When the wicked close in on me to destroy
me, when my enemies attack me, they will
become weak and will fail.
Even when a mighty army rises against me,
my heart will not be afraid. Even if they start
a battle against me, I will be confident.
One thing I have asked of the Lord, and this
will I seek after: that I may live in the house
of the Lord all the days of my life; that I may
delight in the Lord and may meditate in his
temple.
He has hidden me in his place of shelter, and
when evil comes, he will hide me in the
secret place of his shelter.
He has lifted me up on a rock, and now he
has lifted up my head above my enemies. I
have praised his name before the people, and
have offered up in his house of meeting a
sacrifice of jubilation: I will sing, and recite a
psalm to the Lord.
Lord, listen to my cry to you: Have mercy on
me and hear me.
My heart responds to you; my face has
sought you out. I will still seek your face,
Lord.
Do not turn your face from me; do not turn
me away in anger.
Be my helper, do not forsake me; do not
despise me, God my Savior.
Even if my father and my mother leave me,
the Lord will always hold me.
Teach me, Lord, how to live in your way,
and guide me in the right path, because my
enemies want me to fall.
Do not deliver me over to the will of those
who trouble me, for they speak lies against
me and prepare to do violence against me.
But I am certain that I will see the good things
of the Lord right now, while I am living.

I will wait patiently for the Lord, and be
brave and take courage. Yes, I will wait for
the Lord. (Psalm 27)
Anthem: I will see the good things of the
Lord right now, while I am living.
V. The righteous will live in endless joy,
R. And will not dread the future.

Our Father

Pater noster

Our Father,
who are in heaven,
hallowed be your name.
Your kingdom come,
your will be done on earth
as it is in heaven.
Give us this day
our daily bread, and
forgive us our sins as we
forgive those who sin
against us.
And do not lead us into temptation,
but deliver us from evil. Amen.

Reading IV: How many are my sins?

Day Six
Lectio IV: Quantas habeo
Lord, where are you? Why do you hide your face from me?

How many are my sins? Show me my crimes
and offenses.
Why do you hide your face, and consider me
your enemy?
Will you show your power in carrying away
leaves in the wind, or blowing away the dry
straw?
You write bitter things against me, and con-
sume me because of the sins of my youth.
You put my feet in the stocks, after observing
all my paths and considering the steps of my
feet,
I who am to be consumed as rottenness, and
as a garment that is eaten by moths.
(Job 13:23–28)

V. Woe is me, Lord,
for I have sinned.
What should I do?
Where should I flee
but to you, my God?
Have mercy on me
when I come to my last days.
R. My soul is greatly troubled,
but you, Lord, succor me
[Repeat] When I come to my last days.

Reading V: Man, born from a woman

Man, born of a woman, lives only for a
short time and is filled with sorrow—
he blossoms like a flower and is destroyed,
and flees as a shadow, never continuing in
the same state.
Do you think it right to stare at such a one,
and to bring him into judgment before you?
Who can cleanse those who are conceived in
sin? Only you, Lord!
Man lives only a short time; only you know
the number of his months—you have
appointed his bounds that cannot be passed.
Depart a little from him so that he may rest,
until the longed-for end of his day has come,
like that of a hired laborer. (Job 14:1–6)
V. Lord, do not remember my sins when you
come into your kingdom.
R. Lord, my God, may I find pleasure in
your sight
[Repeat] When you come into your kingdom.

Reading VI: Who will grant this to me?

Who will grant this to me, that you will protect me in the place of the dead, and hide me
till your fierce anger passes, and appoint me
a time when you will remember me?

Lectio V: Homo natus de muliere

My present life is miserable.

Lectio VI: Quis michi hoc tribuat

Call to me, Lord, and I will
answer.

Will I live again even after I die? I expect this struggle to continue until my change comes.
You will call me, and I will answer you; you will reach out your right hand to the work of your hands.
You have numbered my steps; but spare my sins. (Job 14:13–16)
V. Lord, do not condemn me after my death; make me to be worthy in your sight.
Therefore I beg you
by your majesty, for you are God,
to take away my wickedness.
R. Furthermore, God, wash me from my unrighteousness, for I have sinned against you and you alone.
[Repeat] Therefore I beg you by your majesty, for you are God, to take away my wickedness.

Third Prayer of Mourning

(NOCTURN)

The third set of prayers of mourning weaves in and out of despair and hope, and climaxes in the great cry of Job, "I know that my Redeemer lives, and in the last day, he will stand on the earth."

- *Retreat*: When you are praying the Prayers for a Time of Grief in a one-day retreat setting, pray this Third Prayer at 3 P.M.
- *Weekly Cycle*: When you are following a weekly cycle, pray the Third Prayer on Friday.
- *Thirty-day Cycle*: When you are praying the thirty-day cycle, follow the directions for daily prayer located in the right-hand column.

I waited patiently for the Lord

I waited patiently for the Lord, and he
heard me.

He heard my prayers, and brought me out of
the depths of my misery. He set my feet on a
rock and directed my steps.

And he put a new song into my mouth, a
song to our God. Many will see and fear,
and they will trust in the Lord.

Blessed is the one whose trust is in the name
of the Lord, and who has not loved vanity
and folly.

You have multiplied your wonderful works,
Lord, my God, and no one is like you. If I
declared and spoke them, they would be
multiplied above numbering.

You did not want sacrifice and offering; but
you have opened my ears. You did not
require burnt offering and sin offering, so
then I said, "See, I am coming." In the head
of the book it is written of me that I should
do your will. My God, I have desired your
will, and your law is in the midst of my
heart.

I have declared your righteousness in the
great assembly. I will not keep silent, as you
know, Lord.

I have not hidden your justice within my
heart; I have declared your truth and your
salvation. I have not concealed your mercy
and truth from the great assembly.

Lord, do not withhold your tender mercies
from me; your mercy and truth have always
upheld me.

For evils without number have surrounded
me; my sins have overtaken me, and I am not
able to see. They are more numerous than
the hairs of my head, and my heart fails me.

Day Seven
Expectans, expectavi

Lord, you have heard my
prayers; deliver me and make
me whole again.

Lord, be pleased to deliver me; Lord, look
down to help me.
Let those who seek after my soul be confused
and ashamed together. Let those who desire
me to be captured by evil be turned back-
ward and be ashamed.
Let those who say to me, "'What is happening to you is good!" be immediately confused.
Let all who seek you rejoice and be glad in
you, and let all who love your salvation say
always, "The Lord be magnified!"
Since I am a beggar and poor, let the Lord
show care for me. You are my helper and my
protector: My God, come quickly. (Psalm 40)

Blessed is the one who cares

Blessed is the one who cares about the needy
and the poor; the Lord will deliver him in the
evil day.
The Lord protects and gives him life, and
makes him blessed on the earth while not
delivering him into the hands of his enemies.
The Lord helps such people when in sorrow
and restores them when in sickness.
I said, "Lord, be merciful to me. Heal my
soul, for I have sinned against you."
My enemies have spoken evil against me:
"When will he die and his name perish?"
And when my enemies come to see me, they
lie: Their hearts are full of sin. When they
leave, they spread their lies and sin.
All my enemies gossip about me; they devise
evil tricks against me.
They determine to lie about me, saying that I
will never rise out of my bed again.
For even my friend, whom I trusted, who ate
my bread, has worked against me.
But Lord, have mercy on me, and raise me

Day Eight
Beatus qui intelligit
Lord, be present to me in this
time of sorrow.

up again, that I may repay them.
By this I know that you are pleased with me,
because my enemy will not rejoice in triumph
over me.
But you have upheld me by reason of my
integrity, and have established me in your
presence forever.
Blessed be the Lord, the God of Israel, for all
eternity. Amen and amen. (Psalm 41)

Just as the deer

Just as the deer thirsts for the streams of
water, my soul, too, thirsts for you, God.
My soul has thirsted after you, the strong
and living God. When will I come and
appear before you?
I have fed on my tears day and night, while
others say to me all day long, "Where is
your God?"
These things I remember, and pour out my
soul, for I used to go into the place of the
wonderful tabernacle, to the house of God,
with the voice of joy and praise, hearing the
noise of the multitude feasting.
Why is my soul sad? And why does it trouble me? Hope in God, for I will again give
praise to him; he is my salvation.
My soul is troubled within me: Therefore I
will remember you from the land of Jordan
and Hermon, from the little hill.
Deep calls to deep at the sound of your
water floods. All your breakers and billows
have passed over me.
In the daytime the Lord commands his
mercy; at night, his song is with me, a prayer
to the God of my life.
I will say to God: "You are my support. Why
have you forgotten me? And why do I go
into mourning, while my enemy afflicts me?"
While my bones are broken, my enemies who

Day Nine
Quemadmodum
In spite of my pain, I will praise
you, God.

trouble me taunt me; they say to me all day long, "Where is your God?"
Why are you sad, my soul? And why are you so upset within me? Hope in God, for I will yet give praise to him, my salvation and my God. (Psalm 42)

Reading VII: My spirit

My spirit is sad; my days are coming to an end, and only the grave remains for me.
I have not sinned, and my eye watches the deeds of the evil ones.
Deliver me, Lord, and set me beside you so that no one may harm me.
My days have passed away, my thoughts are no more, my heart is troubled.
They have turned night into day, saying that in the midst of darkness the light is near again.
If I make the grave my home, and make my bed in darkness;
if I say to rottenness, "You are my father," to worms, "my mother" and "my sister";
where is then my hope, and who considers my patience? (Job 17:1–3, 11–15)
V. The dread of death troubles me every day, for if I sin and do not repent,
in hell there is no redemption:
Have mercy on me, God,
and save me.
R. God, in your name, keep me safe,
And by your truth, deliver me.
[Repeat] For in hell there is no redemption:
Have mercy on me, God, and save me.

Reading VIII: My bones cling to my skin

My bones cling to my skin and my flesh, and nothing but lips are left around my few teeth.

Day Ten
Lectio VII: Meus spiritus
The death of my loved one makes me realize my own impending death.

Day Eleven
Lectio VIII: Pelli mee
I and my loved one will rise from the dead.

Have pity on me, have pity on me, at least
you, my friends, because the hand of the
Lord has touched me.
Why do you persecute me like God, and
revel because of my dying flesh?
Who will allow my words to be written?
Who will grant that they may be written
down in a book,
with an iron pen and in a plate of lead, or
else be graven with an instrument in flint
stone?
For I know that my Redeemer lives, and in
the last day he will stand on the earth.
And I will be clothed again with my skin;
and in my flesh I will see my God,
whom I myself will see, and my eyes will
behold, and not another. This is my hope.
(Job 19:20–27).
V. Lord, grant him/her endless rest, and may
everlasting light shine on them.
R. Lord, you raised Lazarus from the grave:
Grant them rest.
[Repeat] And may everlasting light shine on
them.

Reading IX: Why did you bring me out of the womb?

Why did you bring me out of the womb? I
wish I had died before anyone saw me!
I should have been as if I had not been, car-
ried from the womb to the grave.
Won't my few days be ended shortly? Let me
have a little bit of cheer, before I go and
return no more. I am going to a land that is
dark and covered with the mist of death,
a land of misery and darkness, where there is
the shadow of death, and no order, but everlasting horror dwells. (Job 10:18–22)

Lectio IX: Quare de vulva

Lord, I'm in touch with my
sorrow once again.

V. Lord, deliver me from endless death in that dreadful day when the heavens and the earth will be destroyed, when you will come on the earth with fire.

R. For that day is a day of fierce anger,
a challenge to all wickedness,
a great and better day
when the heavens and the earth will be
destroyed.

V. Therefore, what will you say,
most wretched penitent,
what will you see and what will you do,
when you show forth no goodness before so
great a judge, when you come to death in a
world of fire?

R. No, Christ, we ask you,
we beg you, have mercy on us! We plead
that you will come to those who are lost,
and that you will be unwilling to damn those
whom you have bought:
*When you will come to judge the world
by fire.*

V. Redeem the souls that weep without end.
Those who weep without end walk in dark-
ness; and each of them says, Woe! Woe!
Woe! How great will be the darkness:
*When you will come to judge the world
by fire.*

R. God, you who are the maker of all creatures, you who formed me from the earth
and with your own blood have bought me:
Redeem my body right now,
and may it rise out of the tomb
on the day of doom.
Hear me! Hear me!
Command that my soul be put in the bosom
of Abraham, the patriarch:

When you will come to judge the world
by fire.
V. Lord, deliver me from the pain of hell,
you who broke the back of Satan and visited
hell and sent the light of your mercy
to those who lived in darkness.
R. We cry aloud and say,
"You are our redeemer,
you have come to us,
you have broken the back of Satan,
you have visited hell,
you have given light
and mercy to those
who were in the pain of darkness."

CONTINUE WITH PRAISE

In Praise

(IN LAUDIBUS)

The agony of death and distressful situations leads us to a deeper relationship with God, a relationship of praise. Our prayer is, "Restore unto me the joy of my salvation," as we turn from a primary focus on ourselves to meditate on God, the sovereign Lord of history.

- *Retreat*: When you are praying the Prayers for a Time of Grief in a one-day retreat setting, pray In Praise at 6 P.M.
- *Weekly Cycle*: When you are following a weekly cycle, pray In Praise on Saturday.
- *Thirty-Day Cycle*: When you are praying the thirty-day cycle, follow the directions for daily prayer located in the right-hand column.

Have mercy on me, God

Have mercy on me, God, according to your great love. According to the vast number of your tender mercies, blot out my gross injustice.

Wash me clean from my evil deeds, and cleanse me from my sin.

For I know the extent of the evil I have done, and my sin is always before me.

Against you only have I sinned, and I have done evil before you: You are justified in your words, and blameless when you pronounce judgment.

For I was conceived in gross injustice: and my mother conceived me in sin.

For you have loved truth: You have made manifest to me the mysteries of your wisdom.

Sprinkle me with hyssop, and I will be clean: Wash me, and I will be made whiter than snow.

My ears will be filled with joy and gladness, and my bones that have been humbled will rejoice.

Turn your face away from my sins, and blot out all my evil deeds.

Create a clean heart in me, God, and renew a right spirit within me.

Do not send me away from your face, and do not take your holy spirit from me.

Restore to me the joy of your salvation, and strengthen me with a perfect spirit.

I will teach the unjust your ways, and the wicked will be converted to you.

Deliver me from my blood guilt, God, the God of my salvation, and I will proclaim your justice.

Lord, open my lips, and my mouth will declare your praise.

Miserere mei, Deus

Before praise, confess all unworthiness.

If you wanted me to give sacrifice, I would have given it to you; but you will not be delighted in burnt offerings.

The true sacrifice to God is a broken spirit; a contrite and humble heart, God, you will not turn away.

Lord, be merciful in your good will with Zion, and let the walls of Jerusalem be built up.

Then you will accept the sacrifice of justice, oblations, and whole burnt offerings; then they will sacrifice again. (Psalm 51)

Anthem: My body is bowed down; my mind rejoices in God.

Let a hymn of praise be sung

Day Fourteen
Te decet hymnus
A prayer of praise

God, let a hymn of praise be sung to you in Zion; a vow will be paid to you in Jerusalem.

You who hear my prayer: All people will come to you.

The words of the wicked have overcome us, but you will pardon our sins.

Blessed is the one whom you have chosen: That one will dwell in your courts.

We will be filled with the good things of your house: Holy is your temple, and full of justice.

Hear us, God our Savior: You are the hope of all the ends of the earth, and of the sea far off.

You made the mountains by your strength, being clothed with power: You calmed the depths of the sea, and the noise of its waves, and the tumult of the peoples.

Those who dwell in far-off lands will be in awe of your signs; you will make the coming and going of the morning and of the evening joyful.

You have visited the earth, and have nour-
ished it; you have enriched it in many ways.
The river of God is filled with water: You
have prepared their food; for so you prepare
the earth.
Fill up the streams, and multiply the fruit of
the trees. It will spring up and rejoice in its
showers.
You fill the riverbanks and allow the water
to rise up.
At harvest time, the crops are like your
crown; your carts overflow with abundance.
Even the desert proclaims your goodness,
and the hills are clothed in gladness.
The meadows all have grazing flocks, and
the valleys are filled with grain:
They shout for joy and sing. (Psalm 65)
Anthem: Lord, hear my prayer, and I will
come to you.

God, my God

God, my God, I watch for you at daybreak.
My soul thirsts for you. My body longs
for you,
in a desert land, where there is no path and
no water. So in the sanctuary I have come
before you, to see your power and glory.
For your mercy is better than life: My lips
will praise you.
I will bless you all my life, and in your name
I will lift up my hands.
Let my soul be filled as with marrow and
fatness, and my mouth will praise you with
joyful lips.
When I remember you on my bed, I meditate
on you in the night watches, because you
have been my helper. And I will rejoice under
the cover of your wings. My soul has stayed
near you; your right hand upholds me.
But those who have sought my soul in vain,

Day Fifteen
Deus, Deus meus
O God, I praise you for your
healing.

will go into the lower parts of the earth.
They will be delivered into the hands of the
sword; they will be fed to the foxes.
But the king will rejoice in God; all who
swear by God will glory in him, because the
mouth of those who speak wicked things is
sealed. (Psalm 63).

May God have mercy on us and bless us

Deus misereatur
God, bless me.

May God have mercy on us, and bless us;
may he cause the light of his countenance to
shine upon us, and may he have mercy on us,
that we may know your way upon earth,
your salvation in all nations.
Let the peoples praise you, God; let all
people praise you.
Let the nations be glad and sing for joy, for
you judge the people with justice and direct
the nations upon earth.
Let the peoples praise you, God; let all
people praise you: The earth has yielded its
fruit, and God, our God, will bless us.
God will bless us, and all the ends of the
earth will fear him. (Psalm 67)
Anthem: Lord, by your right hand, you have
picked me up.

I said

Ego dixi
Lord, deliver me from my pain
so I can sing to you.

I said: At the high point of my life I will die.
I am deprived of the rest of my years.
I said: I will not see the Lord God in the land
of the living. I will not see people anymore,
nor live in this world.
My generation is at an end; it is rolled away
from me, like a shepherd's tent. My life is cut
off, as by a weaver; while I was yet but
beginning, he cut me off from the loom.
From morning to night you make an end
of me.

I hoped till morning: He has broken all my bones just like a lion. From morning to night you make an end of me.

I will cry like a young swallow, I will meditate like a dove—my eyes are weak from looking upward. Lord, I am oppressed; be my support.

What can I say? Will he answer me since he has put this upon me? I will wander about all my years.

O Lord, if human life is such, and the life of my spirit is in such things as these, correct me and make me live.

See, in peace my bitterness is most bitter. But you have delivered my soul so that it would not perish; you have cast all my sins behind your back.

For the place of the dead will not thank you, nor will death praise you; those who go down into the pit will not hope for your truth.

The living, only the living will give praise to you, as I do this day: The father will make your truth known to his children.

O Lord, save me, and we will sing our psalms all the days of our life in the house of the Lord. (Isaiah 38:10–20)

Anthem: From the gate of hell, Lord, deliver his/her soul!

Praise the Lord from the heavens

Praise the Lord from the heavens; praise him in the high places.

Praise him, all his angels; praise him, all his hosts.

Praise him, sun and moon; praise him, all stars and light.

Praise him, heavens of heavens; and let all the waters that are above the heavens praise the name of the Lord.

Day Sixteen
Laudate Dominum de cælis
I will praise the Lord.

For he spoke and they were made; he commanded, and they were created.
He has established them for ever, and for
ages of ages; he has made a decree,
and it will not pass away.
Praise the Lord from the earth: you dragons,
and all you who are in the deep part of the
earth;
fire, hail, snow, ice, stormy winds, which
fulfil his word;
mountains and all hills, fruitful trees and all
cedars,
beasts and all cattle, serpents and feathered
fowl,
kings of the earth and all people, princes and
all judges of the earth,
young men and maidens. Let the old with the
younger praise the name of the Lord:
For his name alone is exalted.
The praise of him is above heaven and earth,
and he has made his people strong.
He honors all his godly ones, the children of
Israel, a people who are close to him.
Alleluia. (Psalm 148)

Sing to the Lord

Sing to the Lord a new song;
let his praise be in the church of the saints.
Let Israel rejoice in him who made him, and
let the children of Zion be joyful in their
king.
Let them praise his name with choirs; let
them sing to him with the tambourine and
the psaltery.
For the Lord is well pleased with his people,
and he will give salvation to the meek.
The saints will rejoice in glory; they will be
joyful as they lie in their beds.
The high praises of God will be in their

Cantate Domino

I will sing to the Lord.

mouth and two-edged swords in their hands,
to execute vengeance on the nations,
chastisements among the people:
to bind their kings with fetters, and their
nobles with manacles of iron,
to execute on them the judgment that is
written. This glory is to all his saints.
Alleluia.
(Psalm 149)

Praise the Lord in his holy places

Praise the Lord in his holy places; praise him
in the heavenly arch of his power.
Praise him for his mighty acts; praise him
according to the multitude of his greatness.
Praise him with sound of trumpet; praise him
with psaltery and harp.
Praise him with tambourine and choir; praise
him with strings and organs.
Praise him on high sounding cymbals; praise
him on cymbals of joy.
Let every person praise the Lord. Alleluia.
(Psalm 150)

Laudate Dominum
Let all the earth praise the Lord!

May the Lord God of Israel be blessed

Day Seventeen
Benedictus Dominus Deus Israel
You are to be blessed, Lord, for you have delivered me.

May the Lord God of Israel be blessed,
because he has visited and brought about the
redemption of his people.
He brought salvation to us, in the house of
David, his servant—
as he spoke through the mouth of his holy
prophets of old—
salvation from our enemies and from the
hand of all who hate us,
to perform mercy to our fathers and to
remember his holy covenant,
the oath that he swore to Abraham our
father that he would grant to us,
so that being delivered from the hand of our

enemies, we may serve him without fear, in
holiness and justice before him, all our days.
And you, child, will be called the prophet of
the Highest; for you will go before the face
of the Lord to prepare his ways;
to give knowledge of salvation to his people,
by the forgiveness of their sins;
through the mercy of our God, with which
the sunrise from on high has visited us;
to enlighten those who sit in darkness and in
the shadow of death, to direct our feet into
the way of peace. (Luke 1:68–79)
Anthem: I am the resurrection and the life.
He who believes in me, though dead, will
have life, and all who believe and live in me
will have life forever.
Lord, have mercy on us!
Christ, have mercy on us!
Lord, have mercy on us!

Our Father

Pater noster

Our Father,
who are in heaven,
hallowed be your name.
Your kingdom come,
your will be done on earth
as it is in heaven.
Give us this day
our daily bread, and
forgive us our sins as we
forgive those who sin
against us.
And do not lead us into temptation,
but deliver us from evil. Amen.

Day Eighteen
Exaltabo te, Domine
Therefore, I will exalt your name
forever!

I will extol you, Lord

I will extol you, Lord, for you have upheld
me, and have not allowed my enemies to
rejoice over me.

Lord, my God, I cried to you, and you healed me.

Lord, you have brought forth my soul from the place of the dead: You have saved me from going down into the grave.

Sing to the Lord, you godly ones, and give praise to the memory of his holiness.

For his fierce anger lasts only a short time, but his good will lasts a lifetime. In the evening weeping will have its place, and in the morning, gladness.

And in my prosperity I said, I will never be moved.

Lord, by your favor, you made my mountain stand strong. But you turned away your face from me, and I became troubled.

To you, Lord, will I cry, and I will plead to my God.

What profit is there in my blood, if I go down to the grave? Will the dust praise you or declare your truth?

Lord, hear and have mercy on me; be my helper.

You have turned my mourning into joy; you have loosed my sackcloth and clothed me with gladness,

so that my soul may sing to you, and not be silent. Lord, my God, I will give thanks to you forever. (Psalm 30)

Eternal rest

Requiem æternam

V. Give eternal rest to him, Lord,
R. And everlasting life, grant to him!
V. From the gates of hell,
R. Lord, deliver her soul!
V. I believe in the goodness of the Lord,
R. In the land of the living.
V. Lord, hear my prayer,
R. And let my cry come to you.

Prayer: Lord, incline your ear

Lord, incline your ear to our prayers with
which we plead to you to save the souls of
your servants, both men and women,
whom you have called to pass out of this
world into eternal peace and light,
and into the fellowship of heaven.
By Christ, our Lord. Amen!

God, who calls us to respect our father and mother

God, who calls us to respect our father and
mother:
Have mercy on the souls
of my father and mother,
and forgive them all their sins.
And may we live with them in endless bliss.
Amen!

God, whose nature it is

God, whose nature it is
to have mercy and to spare us,
we pray and beg you
to save the soul of your servant
whom you have called to pass out of this
world,
so that he may not be taken into the hands
of our enemies.
Do not forget him,
but take him up with the holy angels,
and lead him into the presence of eternal life
so that he hopes and believes in you.
Let him be forever glad in the company of
heaven. Amen!

God of mercy

God of mercy,
grant to the soul of your servant
whose memory we make today

Deus, qui patrem et matrem

Deus, cui proprium

Deus indulgenciarum

a time of refreshing,
blissful rest, and
clearness of light.
Amen!

CONTINUE WITH CONCLUDING PRAISE

Concluding Praise

(COMMENDATIONS)

"Commendations" are prayers of "putting into trust," prayers of "giving in charge for care or preservation." The one who is praying has already put the deceased or the painful situation into trust; and now the one praying turns to a series of prayers by which he or she entrusts the person or situation into God's hands and looks to the future, hoping in God.

- *Retreat*: When you are praying the Prayers for a Time of Grief in a one-day retreat setting, pray the Commendations at 9 P.M.
- *Weekly Cycle*: When you are following a weekly cycle, pray the Commendations on Sunday.
- *Thirty-Day Cycle*: When you are praying the thirty-day cycle, follow the directions for daily prayer located in the right-hand column.

Blessed are those whose way is pure

Blessed are those whose way is pure, who walk in the law of the Lord.

Blessed are those who seek his words, who seek him with their whole heart.

They do not sin; they walk in his ways. You have commanded that every part of your laws be kept.

Oh that my feet would follow your paths of righteousness!

Then I will not be ashamed, when I look at all your commandments.

I will praise you with an upright heart, when I have learned your righteous judgments.

I will keep your laws: Do not forsake me! (Psalm 119:1–8)

How can a young person correct his way?

How can a young person correct his way? By observing your words.

With my whole heart I have sought after you; do not let me stray from your commandments.

I have hidden your word in my heart so that I may not sin against you.

You are blessed, Lord: Teach me your laws. With my lips I have pronounced all the ordinances of your mouth.

I have been delighted in the way of your testimonies, as much as in all riches.

I will meditate on your commandments, and consider your ways.

I will delight in your precepts; I will not forget your word. (Psalm 119:9–16)

In quo corrigit
Help me observe your words.

Deal bountifully with your servant

Deal bountifully with your servant; enliven me, and I will keep your word.
Open my eyes, so that I may consider the wondrous things of your law.
I am a stranger on the earth; do not hide your commandments from me.
My soul is breaking with longing for your ordinances, at all times.
You have rebuked the proud; they are cursed who reject your commandments.
Take away from me reproach and contempt, because I have sought after your testimonies.
For rulers sat, and spoke against me, but I, your servant, still studied your law.
For your testimonies are my meditation; your law is my counselor. (Psalm 119:17–24)

My soul clings to the dust

My soul clings to the dust: Revive me according to your word.
I have declared my ways, and you have heard me; teach me your ordinances.
Make me understand the way of your ordinances, and I will be steeped in your wondrous works.
My soul has wept through heaviness; strengthen me according to your word.
Remove from me the way of evil doings, and graciously grant me your law.
I have chosen the way of truth; I have not forgotten your judgments.
I have clung to your testimonies, Lord; do not put me to shame.
I will run the way of your commandments, for you will enlarge my heart. (Psalm 119:25–32)

Day Twenty-one
Retribue servo tuo

Reveal your will to me.

Adhæsit pavimento anima mea

Teach me your ways.

Lord, set your law before me

Lord, set your law before me, and I will
always seek after it.
Give me understanding, that I may observe
your law; I will keep it with my whole heart.
Lead me into the path of your commandments, for I delight in them.
Incline my heart to your testimonies and not
to jealousy of others.
Turn away my eyes so they may not see vanity;
revive me in your ways.
Establish your word to your servant, as that
which promotes reverence for you.
Turn away my disgrace, which I have dreaded,
for your ordinances are good.
See, I have longed for your precepts; enliven
me in your righteousness. (Psalm 119:33–40)

Lord, let your mercy come over me

Lord, let your mercy come over me, your salvation according to your word. So will I
answer those who reproach me, for I trust in
your word.
And do not take the word of truth out of my
mouth, for I have hoped in your precepts. I
will always keep your law, forever and ever.
And I will walk at liberty, because I seek
after your commandments.
I will speak of your testimonies before kings,
and I will not be ashamed.
I will also meditate on your commandments,
which I love.
And I will lift up my hands to your commandments, which I love, and I will be
steeped in your ordinances.
(Psalm 119:41–48)

Day Twenty-two
Legem pone michi, Domine

Make your ways clear.

Et veniat super me

Let me ruminate on your words.

Remember your word

Remember your word to your servant, in which you have given me hope.
In my humiliation, your words comfort me, because your word has revived me.
The proud derided me altogether, but I did not turn away from your law.
Lord, I have remembered your ordinances from of old, and I have been comforted.
I am fiercely indignant because of the wicked who forsake your law.
Your justice is the subject of my song in the house of my pilgrimage.
Lord, I remember your name at night, and keep your law.
I make a habit of remembering your law and seeking after your precepts.
(Psalm 119:49–56)

Lord, you are my portion

Lord, you are my portion. I promise to obey your words.
I seek your favor with all my heart: Have mercy on me according to your word.
I have reflected on my ways, and turned my feet toward your paths.
I am ready, and will not delay in keeping your commandments.
The wicked have surrounded me, but I have not forgotten your law.
I rose at midnight to praise you for your righteous law.
I am friends with all those that fear you, and that keep your commandments.
Lord, the earth is full of your mercy: Teach me your ways. (Psalm 119:57–64)

Day Twenty-three
Memor esto verbi tui
I am keeping your law, help me!

Portio mea, Domine
I long to keep your law.

You have treated your servant well

Lord, you have treated your servant well,
according to your word.
Teach me goodness and discipline and
knowledge, for I believe your commandments.
Before I was humbled I went astray, but now
I keep your word.
You are good, and in your goodness, teach
me your ways.
Arrogant people tell lies about me, but I will
still seek your commandments with my
whole heart.
Their hearts are hard, but I delight in
your law.
It is good for me to have been humbled, so
that I may learn your ways.
The law of your mouth is more precious to
me than thousands of pieces of gold and
silver. (Psalm 119:65–72)

Your hands made me

Your hands have made me and formed me;
give me understanding, that I may learn your
commandments.
Those who fear you will see me and be glad,
because I hope in your word.
Lord, I know that your judgments are
righteous, and that in your truth you
humbled me.
Let your mercy be for my comfort, just as
you have promised.
Give your mercies to me, that I may live, for
I delight in your law.
Let the proud be ashamed, because they
harmed me without cause: But I will still
turn to your precepts.
Let those who fear you turn to me, and those
who know your testimonies.

Bonitatem facisti cum
Teach me to be disciplined.

Manus tue fecerunt
Let me be a testimony to your
words.

Let my heart be pure in your statutes, that I
may not be ashamed. (Psalm 119:73–80)

My soul longs for your salvation

Day Twenty-five
Deficit salutare tuum
Lord, I have failed you again.

My soul longs for your salvation, and I have
waited for your word.
My eyes search for your word: When will
you comfort me?
I have become like a wineskin in the smoke,
yet I have not forgotten your decrees.
How long will I, your servant, live? When
will you punish those who persecute me?
The wicked tell lies about me that are not
your truth.
All your statutes are truth. They persecute
me unjustly; help me, Lord!
They almost destroyed me, but I did not forsake your precepts.
Revive me and be merciful to me, so that I
may keep the testimony of your mouth.
(Psalm 119:81–88)

Lord, your word is forever

**In æternum, Domine,
verbum tuum**
Your law remains forever,
whether I fail or not.

Lord, your word is forever settled in heaven.
Your faithfulness is for all generations. You
created the earth, and it continues in your
care.
At your decree, the day begins: For all things
serve you.
If I had not delighted in your law, I would
have perished.
I will not forget your precepts, for by them
you have given me life.
I am yours: Save me, for I seek your ways.
The wicked have waited for me to destroy
me, but I will consider your testimonies.
Perfection has its limits, but your commands
have no limit. (Psalm 119:89–96)

How I love your law

How I love your law, Lord! I meditate on it all day long.

Your commandments have made me wiser than my enemies, for they are ever with me.

I understand more than all my teachers, because I study your decrees.

I have more knowledge than the elderly, because I have observed your command-ments.

I have kept my feet from evil ways, so that I may instead keep your words.

I have not departed from your laws, because you yourself have taught me.

Your words are sweet to my taste, sweeter than honey to my mouth!

From your commandments I have under-standing; therefore I hate the way of evil.
(Psalm 119:97–104)

I want to meditate on your law day and night.

Your word is a lamp to my feet

Lucerna pedibus

Your word is a lamp to my feet, and a light to my path.

I swear and am determined to keep your righteous judgments.

Lord, I have been humbled; revive me according to your promise.

Receive praise from my mouth, Lord, and teach me your judgments.

I constantly take my life into my own hands, but I have not forgotten your law.

The wicked have set traps for me, but I have not strayed from your ways.

I have inherited your testimonies forever, because they are the joy of my heart.

I have inclined my heart to obey your laws forever, even to the end.
(Psalm 119:105–112)

Your law lightens my path.

I hold the wicked in hatred

I hold the wicked in hatred, but I love your law.

You are my hiding place and my protector, and I hope in your word. Depart from me, evildoers, that I may study the commandments of my God.

Give me strength according to your promises, that I may live; and do not allow my hopes to be shattered.

Uphold me, so that I may be safe, so that I may meditate on your truths.

You reject those who do not keep your laws, for they are unjust in their ways.

You destroy the sinners, but I have loved your truths.

I tremble at your ways, and fear your judgments.

(Psalm 119:113–120)

I have done justly

I have done justly; do not hand me over to those who hate me.

Strengthen me; do not let the proud destroy me.

My eyes fail with longing for your salvation, and for your righteousness.

Give me mercy, and teach me your ways.

I am your servant: Give me understanding, that I may know your testimonies.

Lord, it is time to act, for they have broken your law.

Therefore I love your commandments more than gold, more than fine gold.

Therefore I esteem your commandments as right; I hate every wicked way.

(Psalm 119:121–128)

Iniquis odio habui
I don't join with the wicked.

Feci iudicium
Help me to always affirm your commandments.

Your testimonies are wonderful

Your testimonies are wonderful; therefore my soul keeps them.
The entrance of your words gives light, and understanding to the simple.
Lord, I thirst for your commandments.
Look on me and have mercy on me, according to your manner toward those who love your name.
Direct my steps according to your word, and do not let evil have power over me.
Redeem me from the oppression of men, so that I may keep your commandments.
Make your face shine upon your servant, and teach me your statutes.
My eyes shed springs of water, because they do not keep your law. (Psalm 119:129–136)

You are just, Lord

You are just, Lord, and your judgments are right.
Your testimonies are righteous, and your ways are truth.
My zeal has consumed me, because my enemies have forgotten your words.
Your word is very pure; therefore your servant loves it.
I am despised by many; but I do not forget your precepts.
Your righteousness is forever; and your law is truth.
I am anguished and troubled, yet I delight in your commandments.
Your testimonies will forever be righteous; give me understanding, that I may live. (Psalm 119:137–144)

Mirabilia testimonia tua, Domine
Your commandments are meant for my good.

Day Twenty-eight
Iustus es, Domine
Your fairness is expressed in your commandments.

I cried out with my whole heart

I cried out with my whole heart: Hear me,
Lord! I will observe your commandments.
I cried to you: Save me, and I will keep your
testimonies.
I rise early in the morning and cry out,
because I hope in your word.
My eyes seek you all through the night, so
that I might meditate on your word.
Lord, hear my voice according to your
loving-kindness; revive me according to your
ordinances.
Those who persecute me are near; but they
are far from your law.
Lord, you are near, and all your command-
ments are truth.
From the beginning I have known your truths,
that you have founded them for eternity.
(Psalm 119:145–152)

Clamavi in toto corde meo

Confirm your laws in my life.

See my humiliation

See my humiliation, and deliver me, for I do
not forget your law.
Defend and redeem me; revive me according
to your word.
Sinners are far from salvation, because they
do not seek your statutes.
Lord, your mercies are great; revive me
according to your ordinances.
There are many who persecute me, but I do
not forsake your testimonies.
I despise evildoers, because they do not keep
your word.
Consider how I love your commandments,
Lord: Revive me according to your
loving-kindness.
The sum of your word is truth; all your
righteous judgments endure forever.
(Psalm 119:153–160)

Vide humilitatem

Lord, let me never forget your
commandments.

Princes persecute me without cause

Princes persecute me without cause, but my heart stands in awe of your word.
I rejoice at your words, as one who has found a great treasure.
I hate falsehood; but I love your law.
Seven times a day I give praise to you, because of your righteous ordinances.
Those who love your law have great peace; nothing causes them to stumble.
Lord, I look for your salvation, and I keep your commandments.
I keep your testimonies, and I love them greatly.
I have kept your precepts and testimonies; all my ways are before you.
(Psalm 119:161–168)

Lord, let my cry come before you

Lord, let my cry come before you; give me understanding according to your word.
Let my earnest request come before you; deliver me according to your word.
My lips will sing praise, for you teach me your ways.
My tongue will sing of your word, because all your commandments are righteousness.
Let your hand help me, for I have chosen your precepts.
I long for your salvation, Lord, and I delight in your law.
Let my soul live that it may praise you, and let your ordinances help me.
I have gone astray like a lost sheep; come and find your servant, for I do not forget your commandments. (Psalm 119:169–176)

Day Twenty-nine
Principis persecuti sunt me gratis

Even though I am persecuted, I will keep your commandments.

Intret deprecatio

Let me never forget your commandments.

Lord, you have searched me

Lord, you have searched me, and known me; you know my sitting down, and my standing up.

You know my thoughts from afar; you examine my path and my lying down.

You are aquainted with all my ways; for there is no speech of mine you do not already know.

Lord, you know all things, the new and old; you have formed me, and created me with your hands.

Such knowledge is too wonderful to me; it is too high, and I cannot comprehend it.

Where can I go to escape your Spirit? Or where can I flee from your presence?

If I ascend into heaven, you are there; if I descend into the place of the dead you are present.

If I take the wings of the morning, and dwell in the deepest parts of the sea,

even there your hand will lead me, and your right hand will hold me.

If I say: "Surely darkness will cover me, and night will be my light,"

even darkness is not dark to you, and night will be as bright as the day; darkness and light are alike to you.

For you created me; you formed me in my mother's womb.

I will praise you, for I am fearfully and wonderfully made; how wonderful are your works.

My frame was not hidden from you, when you made me in secret and formed my substance in the lower parts of the earth.

Your eyes saw my unformed being, and in your book every day of my life was written before I was even made.

Day Thirty
Domine, probasti me

Thank you Lord, for leading me into the way of your truth.

Your thoughts, God, are precious to me, and vast. If I could count them, there would be more than the sand. When I awake, I am still with you.

Oh, that you would slay the wicked, God: Get away from me, you bloodthirsty people! They speak of you with evil words and take your name in vain.

Do I not hate them, Lord, who hate you? And am I not grieved because of their words against you?

I hate them with a complete hatred; to me they are enemies.

Search me, God, and know my heart; examine me, and know my thoughts.

And see if there is any evil in me; and lead me in the everlasting way. (Psalm 139)

V. Endless rest, give to him, Lord,

R. And everlasting light to lighten them.

V. From the gates of hell,

R. Lord, deliver her soul!

V. I believe in the goodness of the Lord,

R. In the land of the living.

V. May they rest in peace.

R. Amen!

Prayer: To you, Lord, we commend

Orisun: Tibi, Domine, comendamus

To you, Lord, we commend the souls of your servants, both men and women,

so that being dead to the world they may live to you.

And all of the sins they have done in this world—

wash them away by the forgiveness of your most merciful pity.

By Christ, our Lord. Amen.

HERE END THE COMMENDATIONS
[AND THE MEDIEVAL PRAYER-BOOK PROPER]